YOUR DIVINE LENS:
A PRESCRIPTION FOR
SOULFUL LIVING

THE SECRET TO FINDING PURPOSE, HEALING GRIEF AND LIVING IN ALIGNMENT WITH YOUR SOUL.

By SUE FREDERICK,
AUTHOR OF *BRIDGES TO HEAVEN: TRUE STORIES OF LOVED ONES ON THE OTHER SIDE*

WWW.YOURDIVINELENS.COM

When I'm on path and in alignment with divine order, I feel of use to the greater message, the larger truth, the highest good. Love moves through me like a ray of light piercing everything, a laser beam opening my heart. I just finally get out of the way.

When I forget about divine order, nothing makes sense. My sadness is legendary. My hunger is hopeless. Heartbreak brings me to my knees in despair. Everyone betrays me; my mother, brother, sister, lover, friend. I'm a boat without a mooring. Fear blocks my inner voice. My mind tricks me. I let it.

When I remember to throw out the ego lens and reach for my divine lens, I see the loving God-ness of our universe. Sacred wisdom once again pours through me, showering the world in diamonds - each one forged from the fire of tremendous loss. Forgiveness abounds. I'm held by the angels.

To all of you: Everyone I've loved and been loved by, wounded and been wounded by - you're all my Divine Lens teachers! I honor you for the perfect lessons you've handed me at the exact moments of my greatest need. How extraordinary Divine Order is! I'm hugging all of you right now – especially Gene, Sarah and Kai – my beloved family.

Contents

PREFACE

I've been knocked flat – in bed with 103 degrees of fever and a scary cough that leaves me nauseous and unable to eat. This potent combination of high fever and days without food has cleansed my body, shaken my brain, and broken me wide open. Between bouts of fever, I feel newborn as a baby, joyful and grateful to be alive.

Yet it will take my ego mind weeks in bed to fully understand that I've been knocked flat so I would surrender – let go of old patterns and embrace new realizations, download my next lessons from the divine - and that these new transmissions will take my soul and my work to the next level.

During one memorable night when the fever rose above 103, the thin veil lifted, and I had a vision of our planet on its evolutionary journey of consciousness awakening.

There was a moving river of light spreading around the globe, one light sparking another and another until bands of illumination circled the entire planet- enlightening the dark crevices.

Suddenly I realized that this was the story of human evolution - sparking from one light of divine consciousness into billions and billions of lights gradually overcoming darkness. It was clear how much more light there is in our world than darkness, and I felt assured that light is winning - no matter how tragic the news may seem, or what new events unfold in the future.

This fever-fueled vision inspired me with new ideas and concepts to write about. Much of what I dreamt and understood that night I couldn't remember when I first woke up. I did remember my sense of "knowing" that all is well in the world and moving in the right direction.

For days I struggled to articulate these ideas to family and friends. I felt transformed from this out-of-body experience and was reborn into a new level of work.

This work solidified into specific ideas over the next few weeks until I was consumed with the concept of the divine lens vs. the ego lens as our two primary ways of perceiving events in our lives.

This new concept and how to reap the benefits of Divine Lens viewing is what this book is all about.

INTRODUCTION

You either believe in divine order or you don't. It's an all or nothing thing. Either you're aware that all events occur for your soul's growth, your highest good, and the highest good of all - or life feels chaotic, painful and meaningless.

Each day provides numerous opportunities to shift back and forth between those two views until you fully align with the view that empowers you most and moves your life in a positive direction. Only then can you fulfill your soul's mission and live up to your greatest potential.

Wearing your divine lens is like putting on a new pair of prescription glasses and suddenly seeing a world you never saw before: the small miracles in everyday life, the divine order behind each challenge, the love hidden in every painful interaction.

For example, when you get a new job, your business becomes successful, you fall in love or have a baby, you may find yourself saying: "Things happen for a reason." You slip on your divine lens at those moments and offer gratitude to a loving God or a benevolent universe that operates for our highest good.

When things aren't going so well; when you lose that great job, when you're facing bankruptcy, your spouse divorces you, or your child dies in a tragic accident you may feel angry at a God who would cause such cruel suffering. Or rage at an unjust universe where tragic events unfold for no apparent reason.

Yet each crisis is your awakening; a fresh opportunity to discover if you're living from your soul's perspective, your divine view, or from your ego self. Once you're aware of these warring perspectives within and their consequences, you can choose to view life through your divine lens. That choice changes everything. For the better.

We may also think of the divine lens like the lens of a camera. We can view the world through a macro lens close-up where we aren't aware of a bigger picture and don't understand where the leaf of a rose petal fits into the larger scope of a rose bush, a rose garden, a region, a country or a world.

This is what we do when we view our greatest pain (a tragic loss of a loved one or the ego-crushing experience of being fired from a great job) as the largest and most significant event in our lives with nothing from past or future to give it larger meaning or reference points. Through this macro view lens we aren't able to understand that our pain is a bump in the road in the long journey of our soul – a challenge perfectly designed to move us into greater spiritual wisdom and higher consciousness for the highest good of all – including the highest good of our departed loved one. We don't see how linked we are to all other souls who also feel great loss and find their way their way through the pain. This microscopic macro view is the ego lens view.

Or we can use the panoramic lens on the camera and suddenly see a larger world with endless life, possibilities and meaning than we can realize when focused on one moment of great pain. We understand our soul story then within this larger panoramic view of all of our shared soul stories. This is our divine lens. It shows connections and threads where our ego lens sees only pain.

We can also imagine using different filters on the camera lens that either highlight the shadows within the frame or highlight the light within the frame. When we're using the ego lens, we see mostly shadow wherever we look. When we're using the Divine Lens, we see light even in the dark corners. This is where our wisdom lives – within the light of the darkest corner of our lives.

Whenever you're afraid, grief stricken, shut down or angry, it's time for realignment with your highest self. The ego self has lied to you and taken you far from who you came here to be. Your ego lens is only revealing a small piece of your story – a moment of utter loss that separates you from your higher self and from the higher selves of others. This separation from soul shows up in your life as fear, confusion, depression, addiction and anger.

Fear, addiction, pain and despair occur when we lose the connection to our higher self, our divinity. Of course, we ALL experience moments of great pain and despair. It's part of our human journey here.

Yet the moment we cry for help from our higher self everything changes. It's as simple as saying: *Please divine guides, God, or higher self help me shift into my soul's wisdom to see the lesson in front of me. Quiet my ego mind and open my heart.*

Take a breath and wait for the shift. Listen to the inner voice that speaks with love and not fear.

At that moment, you're lifted into the divine view of life and reminded that you're a powerful soul who came here on purpose to evolve and help others. Unexpectedly you see divinity in everything; the golden glow of love in each painful and joyful moment. You feel expanded, unafraid, open and clear on how to move forward. Your divine lens is activated.

The ego mind tells you you're here to win, manipulate, accumulate, conquer, protect and defend. The divine lens shows you the grand view of your soul's perspective. It reveals that you agreed to be born into this lifetime to face these exact moments of crisis and view them with love, gratitude and wisdom; to understand the pain of others who may be hurting you; to realize that everyone is doing exactly the best they can given their level of consciousness; and that all is forgiven in the end.

Your divine lens reveals that YOU are a highly evolved soul who intended to shine your wisdom on the painful dark moments of your life and to help others do the same. YOU came here to shine love on your fear; to pour light on your greatest pain.

Every single day of your lifetime has been perfectly designed to help you remember your divinity and shift out of the frightened ego view that's rooted in our physical experience of being human.

In one moment of recognizing this, one heart-opening shift of perspective, your life changes, your soul speaks up, and your next step is revealed.

PART ONE:
THE DISTORTIONS OF
YOUR EGO LENS

At this very moment, your divine self is battling your ego self to determine how you'll experience this day. Your divine self whispers: "This is your greatest moment. Choose love over fear. Step into the light and become the source of love for everyone."

Your ego self whispers: "I'm not good enough or strong enough. Life is unfair. I'm in too much pain."

Today, in spite of whatever challenges you face, you can gain a new and enlightening perspective by putting on your "divine lens." When you embrace this new perspective, it empowers you to live everyday in alignment with your soul's wisdom.

When you perceive life this way for a few minutes each day, awareness will begin to grow within you until your life is moving forward gracefully, your relationships and career are thriving, and your pain is diminished. This is the gift of your divine lens.

I personally believe that once you experience the rich benefits and the mind-altering shift of your divine lens, you'll never leave home with it. You'll react differently to every challenging moment as you learn to remove your ego lens and slip on your divinity. It truly changes everything.

Ego Lens or Divine Lens?

The most wonderful thing about being human is our ability to choose. In this earthly realm, we're allowed to experience the perfect combination of destined soul mission and free will - every moment of our lives.

We each come here with a great soul intention to live up to our greatest potential, line our lives up with our highest self, and do great work that helps others. Yet we also hit bumps in the road; loss, illness, financial challenges, childhood pain and relationship turmoil.

Free will allows us to decide exactly how we'll view each challenge and how we'll use every gift we've brought with us. No one else chooses our viewpoint for us. We are the ones who determine how we view our life story.

We can choose to view this world as only a physical world with random tragedies and meaningless coincidences. Or we can choose to view life through the eyes of our soul.

When we align our ego mind with the wisdom of our soul – we see things differently. Light pours through us and reveals the hidden beauty of each moment. We see that each challenge was perfectly designed for our highest good before this lifetime began. We understand that the purpose of each bump in the road has been to help us grow and awaken - which is the primary reason we incarnated into this physical realm.

Life on earth is a human consciousness experiment that we've all agreed to participate in. We're expanding consciousness into this dense realm; and this evolutionary process has been going on for billions of years.

I

Spiritual Crisis:
Are you Religious, Spiritual,
Both or Neither?

From my earliest memory I loved going to Catholic Church. I felt God's presence amongst the towering statues, flickering candlelight, pungent incense, and the stained glass windows that depicted a compassionate Jesus placing healing hands on a child or the barefoot St. Francis of Assisi kneeling in prayer while birds rested peacefully on his shoulders. These loving deities filled my dreams and spoke to me when I prayed.

But Mother Mary with her long hair and flowing blue gowns was my constant companion. I prayed the rosary to her nearly everyday and knew without doubt that she was my loving mother. I turned to her in every childhood moment of pain and her graceful presence comforted my heart.

As I grew older I began to understand the beliefs and dogmas of the Catholic Church: the burden of "original sin" that I was born with, the poison of "mortal sin" that could send me to burn in hell forever, and the persistent need for daily penance to atone for sins and embrace the suffering of the cross.

My blossoming adolescent sensuality, according to the nuns, was a perilous slide towards mortal sin. In daily religion class, we were instructed to avoid looking at our own bodies when we bathed for fear of slipping into mortal sin and everlasting damnation. As much as we prayed, went to Mass, and devoted our lives to Jesus and Mary, one tiny mistake could ruin everything, according to the priests and nuns.

These Catholic dogmas grew increasingly impossible to align with. They created a growing rift between my religion and my inner knowingness. Eventually my discomfort with the teachings of these Catholic elders caused me to search for new answers that aligned with a forgiving God whom I knew in my heart did not punish. I loved God and Mary with all my heart. Their daily presence in my life did not line up with the punishing God described in Catholic dogma.

My soul refused to believe that all souls who were not Catholic (Hindus, Buddhists, Jews, Muslims, Presbyterians, Episcopalians, Baptists, Methodists and on) were condemned to hell for eternity. This never resonated as true for me. I would've been willing to forego sex forever if God demanded that of me, but I simply knew in my gut that every being on earth had a beautiful soul and was doing their best. This I knew for sure when I trusted my inner wisdom.

When I left home for college in 1969, a new world opened up. I saw fliers for Theosophy, yoga, and meditation classes on campus bulletin boards and was instantly drawn to learn what those things were about.

These classes launched a life long journey of spiritual exploration – complete with residencies in New Age studies, Buddhist and Hindu ashrams, Unity Churches, metaphysical classes, and the school of nature. During my 20s, I lived outdoors, absorbing the spiritual truths in nature, teaching mountaineering for Colorado Outward Bound School for months at a time. I was drawn to places and people that exhibited a spiritual wisdom I wanted to absorb.

From my journey, I've come to believe that religion is a starting place – not a destination. A church or dogma may launch our spiritual exploration, but religion's main purpose is to hook us up to the divine, to help us experience something beyond the physical world, to get us asking the great questions: Who am I? Why am I here? Where do I go when I die?

Once religion has gotten us to this point, we need to find our own personal connection to the divine realms and follow the path that resonates as true, that does not dictate our behavior through fear-based dogma, but instead wraps us in love and wisdom.

We can do both. We can maintain our connection with the religion whose community and sacred traditions comfort us – while also nurturing our own personal spiritual connection to the divine in the manner that feels true to us.

Once you've embraced your spiritual not religious point of view, you've found your soul's reference point. The essential next step is creating a disciplined daily practice of personal connection to the divine. This daily personal practice is something you can do while also following the religious traditions of Judaism, Catholicism, Christianity or whatever community you're comfortable with. It doesn't have to be all or nothing; religion or spirituality. But spirituality does require a daily discipline of connection.

Whether you choose 20 minutes of mantra-based meditation, contemplative prayer, or chanting, your daily spiritual practice is as necessary for a healthy life as brushing your teeth. It's your moment to slip on your divine lens, quiet the ego mind, and connect to your soul's wisdom. A consistent practice allows you to experience the enormous benefits of divine lens viewing - at least once a day.

Your soul knows the difference between fear-based doctrine and enlightened wisdom and will nudge you to run from dogma. Your disillusionment with a church is only the beginning of a spiritual journey. A daily personal practice of sacred connection is required for life in the physical world - where we so quickly forget our divinity.

This juncture is where many people get lost. They feel deceived by religion and mistakenly think God has deceived them, so they turn away from all things sacred. Yet God is embracing them. If they choose to listen to their soul's wisdom they'll remember this. They'll pick up their divine lens.

Sometimes it takes a painful loss, a reinvention point, to re-open our search for spiritual truth. We begin seeking answers again in moments of pain - which eventually leads us away from our comfort zone and into true spiritual awakening. This is the gift of our pain.

Your spiritual awakening

Be wary of any spiritual teaching or teacher who makes you feel afraid or bad about yourself, or doesn't resonate as true. Quiet your mind, listen to your inner wisdom and you'll know the truth.

You're a divine spiritual explorer who came here to evolve and help others. It's your job to cross boundaries, question everything, and search for meaning. If you're living your life in fear and aren't sure what you believe, it's time to break the rules. You have nothing to lose and everything to gain.

If you were taught that God punishes us, condemns us to hell for transgressions, you'll probably hunker down to fit into this fear-based system for much of your life. If you leave your church, you may feel guilt-ridden and believe that now you'll go to hell for breaking the rules. This is your ego mind speaking, not your divine self.

If your parents were punishing and controlling, you may believe that it's your job to obey everyone including the church's laws - unquestionably - because that's what you were raised to do. This is a sign that you've turned away from the voice of your soul's wisdom in order to survive a painful childhood. Your inner wisdom still waits for you. It's the voice of love buried within your heart. Fitting into others' expectations and beliefs is the fastest road to disconnection from your inner wisdom.

God IS love. That's all you need to know. That simple truth contains all the dogma necessary to live your best life and fulfill your soul's mission.

Divine order is always acting in your favor. No matter how shut down or off-path you've been, your soul will create a wake-up call for your highest good. This will arrive as a divorce, bankruptcy, job loss, or loss of a loved one. Suddenly you'll be asking the important questions again and refusing to settle for answers that don't resonate as true. This is your soul taking charge (instead of your ego) and getting your life back on path. Your divine lens has been re-activated.

You might now step out of bounds for the first time in your life and be amazed to discover that you're not condemned to hell.

That instead you feel alive, fearless, loving and joyful. Your inner truth has been rediscovered.

You've re-opened your inner compass – known as intuition. Eventually you're traveling to the edges of the world to know what can be known, to discover the wisdom that can't be learned within the boundaries of convention.

You've found your way home to the divine.

2

SELF DOUBT: HOW THE EGO LENS DESTROYS CONFIDENCE

When we think of being in our ego state, we imagine this means that we're overly confidant, arrogant, and boastful. It's the opposite of this. When we're using the ego lens to view our world, to view any situation, we're looking at ourselves and others as limited beings with limited potential, competing to survive. The ego lens tells us we need to struggle to get what we need because there's never enough to go around and we're never good enough to get it done - so we must be better than everyone else to succeed. The ego lens thrives on seeing differences.

When you allow this view to dominate your life, you pull the plug on your inner wisdom - the source of your personal power. This drains your energy and leaves you defeated and exhausted. The stress of having to be "the best" – which your soul knows is unnecessary and impossible - will push you far from the unique path you came to experience. The ego lens hides the truth. It blocks your ability to clearly see your unique gifts or the gifts of others.

Our ego lens only sees the surface of life. Our divine lens makes no assumptions. It reveals the deeper truth behind every story, the pain hidden in each misbehavior, the soul journey behind every wounded personality. It reveals similarities rather than differences. The divine lens is your prescription for compassion. It aligns you with your soul's wisdom and empowers you to be your greatest self.

The divine lens reveals that you're perfectly who you're supposed to be at this moment - which is exactly as powerful, beautiful and brilliant as you're meant to be today. This perspective allows you to shine - even when your mind tells you that you're inferior, powerless, or not good enough.

The divine lens illuminates each moment of your life with wisdom; it pours light into your wounds. It fills every dark space with love. Wearing your divine lens, you understand that the gifts of others are perfectly unique to them and what their soul came to accomplish. You see that you're absolutely radiant when you speak your soul's truth, share your wisdom, and speak from your heart - not your mind.

Never doubt that your soul would put you anywhere anytime but exactly where you're meant to be for your highest good and the good of others. Your task is to embrace each painful moment and flip it into gratitude for the gift of what you're learning and the gift of knowing that divine order is already helping you move through this perfectly designed lesson.

Whenever you call out to your highest self for guidance, you open to source energy and flawless wisdom. You open your channel of inspiration. Divinity pours through you.

Then you become the goddess, the prince, the golden child. All meaningless ego comparisons fall away, seem ridiculous. You carry the light within. You get the job you're not qualified for, the standing ovation, the partner you thought would never notice you. Your work, which is your holy sacrament, shines with resonance.

This is divine lens living. At it's finest. And it's available to you 24/7. Just for the asking.

If I'm a divine being why do I doubt myself?

If today, your ego mind is tormenting you - saying you've messed up, made wrong choices, ruined relationships, and aren't good enough -reach for your divine lens. It's the antidote to self-doubt.

It reveals the perfection of your soul's journey of evolution in spite of how ego views it or labels it.

Yet since the day you were born, you've been hypnotized into trusting the ego. As a child you were taught: "You don't know the truth. Only those outside of you do." This is the voice of self-doubt - born of the ego and its limited perceptions.

This idea is forced upon everyone who takes a human lifetime. As children, we're taught that our elders know better than us and that we must listen to them and trust them.

Yet children have an inner voice of wisdom. They've recently arrived from the divine realms and their intuition is unrestricted. They may not be able to navigate their physical bodies yet or understand the rules of the society they've incarnated into, but they're filled with inner wisdom, truth and knowingness.

You were also this conscious and aware when you arrived. If your childhood was difficult it means that your soul posse - parents and siblings - were struggling to do what they were capable of understanding as right action - even though you may have suffered because of the their unenlightened behaviors. Your soul agreed to these experiences as part of your higher education. You still had choices within each painful moment.

As a child, your inner voice advised you to stay away from some adults and stay close to others. You sensed energy and navigated through six senses (intuition) rather than five. You were a six-sense being until you stumbled, hit your head, or put your hand on a hot burner and learned that the physical world had different laws than the divine realms, and that you needed to focus on learning the physical laws of survival. This narrowed focus diminished your sensory awareness, by necessity. Intuitive input from your sixth sense took a back seat.

This was all required for learning to live on planet earth, for navigating a clumsy body through the dense energy of gravity. Yet the downside of learning these things was that you began to shut down your inner knowingness – your sixth sense. Advice from well-meaning parents, siblings, teachers, friends, and ministers became too overpowering to ignore.

As expected by your elders, you surrendered to the complete human experience of the ego self - which was very different from your previous existence in the divine realms. You diminished everything about yourself to survive here.

Thus your inner struggle between ego self and divine self began - with the ego self winning as you became more successful at navigating the physical world. This was the natural process of adjusting to life in this realm.

In the early years, you mourned the loss of those divine realms, of your divine self. You felt homesick for something you couldn't quite remember or describe. Your toddler tantrums expressed the frustration of life in a physical body – which was so different from what you remembered.

Your divinity slipped away gradually as you learned the laws of appropriate behavior. The adults around you approved of this transformation. They complimented you for turning into such a well-behaved boy or girl.

You gradually became defined by your environment, shutting out the extra information available from your sixth sense because it was too confusing and unacceptable.

If you were sensitive and not fully shut down to your intuition, you felt confused by the contrast between what your elders advised and what your inner voice longed for. Your longing to reconnect to something you could not quite remember and your urge to follow your own path were powerful.

Because of this longing, you may have chosen to take the path less traveled as soon as you stepped out to live life on your terms. This choice would eventually lead you to a life in alignment with your unique soul mission.

If you followed the path laid out for you by others, you would hit reinvention points later on, possibilities for changing direction. If you listened to your inner wisdom at those turning points, you would also find your way to fulfilling your highest potential. Divine order always provides openings, small miracles, sacred opportunities that show up exactly when we need them to.

But Why Do I Second Guess Myself?

The viewing of your life through ego lens inevitably makes you doubt yourself. If your intention is to speak your soul's truth and share your wisdom, you'll often be misunderstood by others. Your ego will tell you this is because you're a loser and you're too different to fit into or succeed in this world. Once you remember that you carry a light inside of yourself that cannot be diminished, you'll no longer doubt yourself. Your uniqueness is your gift.

Your physical self is part of the reason you struggle so much. Your body is a great weight that you carry in this dimension. Sometimes this heaviness is too much and pulls you away from your divinity. But your body is also a great gift that can be used to connect to the divine.

There are several small steps to help lift you into the higher frequencies. These include: physical movement, getting outside in nature, laughing with others, meditation to quiet the mind, crying to release the pain in your heart, and sending compassion to those who misunderstand you.

Once you remember that you're here to enlighten others and be the teacher, you'll stop being disappointed in those less evolved than you. By aligning with your higher self, you'll see the pain that others carry and you'll become the healer. No one can wound you when you stand in alignment with your soul.

When you allow yourself to be wounded, you sink into the mud of doubt and fear, which is not where you belong and not who you came here to be.

Those less evolved are drawn to you because you carry the light inside. It's because of your open heart, your powerful soul's wisdom, that others who need healing show up in your life. When you allow yourself to be wounded by them, you're throwing your gifts away.

And when they don't react immediately as you'd hoped and step into their divine light, you feel discouraged, or worse, you feel worthless. This only hurts you and pulls you away from your divinity.

Feeling worthless and discouraged is an enormous waste of time for you and for anyone. There is no soul here who is worthless. There is no soul who has any reason to feel discouraged. All is evolving as it should. You are evolving as you should...

The judgments of others reveal infinitely more about them and their willingness to grow than about you. How many lifetimes will it take you to learn this, to see their criticisms and contempt as misunderstandings due to low levels of consciousness - rather than a statement of your worth or value.

Once you absorb this lesson you will never be hindered by criticism from yourself or others again. You'll become the source of loving wisdom for others, and everywhere you walk you'll fill the room with light.

3

Fear: The Favored Lens of the Ego

Love is the ocean. Fear is what we imagine lurking below the surface; the shark circling our legs, the crab biting our toes. Yet we've come here to swim in this ocean of love. Love is the essence of our DNA.

Fear is the creation of the ego mind. We need the ego to survive in this physical world, but it pulls us away from love. The ego doesn't understand love except as something to acquire from others. The ego mind is linear and logical and nothing more.

We connect to love, divinity, intuition, and creativity through the right brain. We arrive in this dense realm fully accessing both sides of the brain, left and right. But as we mature, we're slowly talked out of love. Cultural beliefs and values support left-brain logic dominance over right brain intuition.

Our souls inherently love everything and everyone. Love is the fabric of the higher realms and the energy we're composed of. We're designed to be sources, channels, of infinite divine love. Our minds are simply filters to help us navigate this physical world. But once we arrive here, we're taught to worship the mind over the heart and soul.

Our left-brain ego-driven world tells us that receiving love is the priority and the key to happiness. This is completely backwards. True happiness only exists when we allow ourselves to channel in divine love for others, to become a source of infinite love and forgiveness.

Once we realize that quieting the ego mind, the left-brain, allows us to love fearlessly, we've found the key to a meaningful, joyful life. We've realigned with soul.

The soul is not designed to take from others. The soul is designed to be the channel of divinity, grace and light for everyone, to forgive fearlessly. Love is the only antidote to fear. When you're afraid of anything or anyone, it means your ego voice has the upper hand and has drowned out the voice of your soul. You're out of alignment with divinity.

When love is not given freely, your energy becomes stagnant which creates neurosis, dependency, psychosis and fear. These are symptoms of misalignment with higher self, of spiritual constipation.

Choose one person in your life to begin practicing unconditional love. Send pure love and gratitude to them for several minutes a day. Don't ask for or expect anything in return. Requiring love in return destroys love. Your mission is to understand your ability to love freely and reawaken your fierce and powerful heart.

This reawakening will transform your life. It'll cure whatever ails you, heal all wounds, and create loving relationships. It will change the way you think and behave towards others. It will shift you directly into your divine lens view and shatter the ego lens.

If you find yourself thinking that someone doesn't deserve your love, or has hurt you too much to forgive, it means you've shifted back into your ego mind and are no longer wearing your divine lens. These are fear beliefs from the ego mind. And they're out of alignment with your highest self and who you came here to be.

Your higher self sees that we're all here on a shared journey of awakening, and that the un-awakened need more love, not less. Pouring love and compassion on those who've hurt you sparks them into higher consciousness eventually. Only when we're all awakened will consciousness shift and the highest realms finally merge with this physical realm to create true perpetual love that shines light into the dark crevices where lost souls have lingered.

Angelic beings have been working towards this goal for eons. At first they worked alone. Now humans have evolved enough to perform angelic duties here on earth, helping transform the dense matter into light.

Jesus, Buddha and many others teachers have brought this message to earth. But our human ego interpretations of their ideas twisted and distorted their original words and turned them into fear-based doctrines and stringent rules that hid their original message of divine love.

We're awakening now, beginning to remember who we are and distancing ourselves from the poison of the ego mind - which destroys the fire of love burning inside all of us. The ego's fear-based reign is never permanent. It never wins in the long run. The soul is infinitely more powerful than the ego. And love trumps all.

Little steps change everything. A lifetime immersed in ego-based living can be shifted with a moment of love and compassion, a moment of seeing a loved one's tragic death as divine order, or parent's betrayal as a symptom of their need for love.

It takes baby steps to break a lifetime pattern of ego and fear-based living. Seeing just one painful moment through your divine lens changes everything.

From my soul to yours...

Fear is the great crippler, the dark force, the energy void. It's the Achilles heel that all humans share. It's what we push against so that we can choose courage and love instead - and light our way through the darkness.

Thank you fear for being such a powerful teacher, for waking me at night with heart tremors, for unplugging me from my source, for taking on the illusion of bills to pay, a business to grow, a book to write, children to provide for, a husband dying of cancer, a boyfriend leaving, and terrifying self doubt. Such magnificent lessons!

God bless you fear, for getting my attention more than everything, more than anyone, more than love, more than joy. You found me when no one else could. You sought me out, pushed me into corners, made me weep, made me angry, and broke me in half. Finally, fear, you broke me wide open.

For that moment of total surrender to the divine, I am deeply grateful. Only then did I embrace my soul and step fully into the light – refusing to ever go back into your dungeon, refusing to be your prisoner again.

Fear, my old friend, I recognize you now when you come to me in the night, disguised as bills, illness, heartbreak, grief or disappointment. – I recognize you, master of disguises. I recognize you by the stirring in my gut as you approach, the quickening of my heart, the frantic pacing of my thoughts. Ah! It is only you!

And you, fear, are not real...

You are the boogeyman I planted in my closet. The one I told to awaken me in the night so I would learn to dance with you instead of cry. So I would learn to use you as fuel to help me reach my next level. So I would see ultimately that you are my friend, my fertilizer, my divine companion on this journey to rediscover my soul.

I embrace you, fear, because without you I would be nowhere. I would never have jumped off my first cliff into the unknown. I would never have stepped into my first terrifying adventure that changed everything. I would never have found my voice. Because without you, fear, I would still be sleeping.

You can stay in the closet or you can dance with me. It makes no difference. My light cannot be diminished. It never could. But it took you showing up for me to discover that.

Now I love you so much, fear, that I can't find you - no matter how hard I look. My love has destroyed you, flooded your darkness, washed away your disguises, illuminated every crevice where you once hid.

When I turn to face you, I only see divine order in your place. I only feel my burning heart pulsing with gratitude, my arms stretching up to grasp the light.

Let me tell you a story...

In the spring of 1976, I was a 25-year-old Montessori pre-school teacher living in Missouri and looking for reinvention. My first love had moved out and broken my heart. I was drowning in self-doubt. When a friend mentioned that he'd once taken an Outward Bound survival course and it had changed his life, I was in.

After a few phone calls to O.B. headquarters in Hurricane Island, Maine I packed some clothes and drove my little Honda Civic across the country for a three-week-long June course on an open pulling boat off the foggy coast of Maine. I'd heard the stories of being dropped off alone on a tiny island for three days with only a tarp and some water. I knew about the required morning jumps from the edge of a 75-foot-cliff into the freezing Maine water where you could die of hypothermia in 20 minutes. I was terrified and elated.

I'd never done anything like this. I'd grown up in the 50s in the conservative south where girls behaved well and men created the rules. I'd found my posse of true friends when I'd dropped out of University of Missouri in 1970 to march against the Vietnam war and ultimately to launch a dream. Mostly disowned by our conservative families because of our alternative beliefs, we worked menial jobs, opened "health-food restaurants," bought land, grew our food, and lived organically before that was a thing. We discussed, debated and practiced new kinds of spiritual awareness such as meditation, metaphysics and living simply. I had completely loved that part of my journey. But the "real" world beckoned as we each awoke to the realities of financial survival on untamed land in the center of Missouri. Most of us left the farm in pursuit of more meaningful careers and the training they required. I'd pursued and become a teacher.

I'd done okay as a Montessori preschool teacher, but it soon felt like it wasn't enough, like I was starving for something more, never having taken my true path – whatever that was to be. And when my first love moved out, I became untethered, without boundaries, adrift. My soul was hungry for new direction; for rebirth. I felt I had nothing to lose.

From the first moment of arrival at Hurricane Island, we were treated like military grunts in basic training, given duffle bags to stuff our few pieces of clothing into, assigned to bunk beds, run through obstacle courses and taught basic nautical navigation with compass and sea charts. We were required to run at least three miles around the island every morning at sunrise, culminating in the morning cliff jump. I'd never run before. I'd been a dancer. This was 1976 – long before the movie Rocky changed our culture, turning us into fist-pumping fitness addicts. I was winded and exhausted from the first step of every early morning run.

I'll never forget my initiation into cliff jumping, as dozens of cold and terrified people just like me lined up to take our turns running and jumping off a cliff that clearly lead to a hideous death far below (either smashed against the rocky shore if we did not leap far enough or drowning in the tumbling waves of the deep blue sea). I was trembling and nauseous with fear as I got closer to the front of the line. But my wise instructor whispered: "Don't think. Just run and jump. Feel the fear and do it anyway."

In that moment, my life truly did begin to change. I took a deep breath, opened my heart and ran for it. I was suddenly soaring over the water screaming, laughing, then underwater fighting for the surface. When I immerged, I heard cheers and felt the most immense joy I'd ever known. Pure elation. I'd done a terrifying and impossible thing and loved it.

For the next three weeks, the hardest weeks of my life thus far, I found myself overcoming fear a thousand times a day. I'd been randomly assigned to a "mobile course" – meaning that after our initial basic training on Hurricane Island, 12 of us lived together on a wooden open pulling boat with two sails and 24 heavy oars – enough for everyone to row endlessly on the windless foggy sea.

Hypothermia was a constant threat as we slept in sleeping bags thrown on top of the oars laid crosswise across the boat. We sailed or rowed from island to island – sailing through storms that left us puking and rowing through windless days for back-breaking hours. When we arrived on an island, we hauled our gear to the beach and instantly went for long runs together.

Our instructors read to us every day and night; inspiring stories of famous adventurers who'd trekked into the unknown to discover new lands or climbed unclimbed peaks in impossible conditions. The message was simple: Human potential is immeasurable and its imagined limits are always being stretched. Step up to your untapped potential. Break through limitations. Fear is simply energy. Use it to move forward.

My instructor was bad-ass and wise all at once. When I lagged behind on a morning run, he would jog beside me whispering about finding my inner strength and not being wimpy. When we rowed around an island to discover a towering 100-foot rock cliff rising straight up from the open sea, he taught us to rock climb. I felt strong and smart on my first-ever climb, with the sea to my back and the promise of heaven above, I stretched and reached and pushed like a dancer on a vertical stage. When I reached the top, my instructor told me that I was a graceful and talented natural climber, and that I was stronger than I knew. I drank his words like water.

I believed my first lover had left me because I wasn't good enough – deeply flawed, too insecure. I was wrapped in self-doubt from childhood, raised by a mother who never knew how to love me, and shamed in a family where my kind of sensitivity, intuition and spiritual awareness was discarded. I was the oldest, and my role was to be perfect and to raise the younger siblings – which I did until the age of 18. That was my job - especially as my mother surrendered to miscarriages and depression. I swore I'd never be like her. But leaving home at 18, I didn't know a single good thing about myself except that I could write.

Alone for three days on that tiny freezing island off the Maine coast, nestled under a flimsy tarp strung between evergreens, as storm after storm washed through, I was terrified at night by the howling wind and pounding waves, the deep black sky, the sense of utter isolation from the world. Left with nothing but my fear and my tears, I began to remember who I was. I found my radiant indestructible soul. I was reborn into someone strong and good. Fear was now my ally. Fear and doubt became my fuel for reinvention.

After that course was over, I returned to Missouri, became an avid rock climber, and worked my way through college to get a degree in psychology and to impossibly become a Colorado Outward Bound mountaineering instructor two years later – which led me on the journey to be who I am today.

When we bravely say yes to life, open our hearts, and jump into the deep blue sea of fear, we emerge stronger than we ever believed we could be, we awaken to our true selves. We shift from ego lens to divine lens, and everything changes for the better.

4

ANGER AND JEALOUSY:
HOW THE EGO FIRES YOU UP

Anger and rage are part of our collective human experience. As our collective consciousness becomes more evolved, we begin to understand that when we stand in anger we see people and events through the ego lens rather than the divine lens.

The ego lens shows us that we're separate from others, disconnected, and victims to those more powerful than ourselves. The ego mind tells us there is injustice in the world; so anger is justified.

This approach to life and to painful events is fine at first. In our youth, we may use anger to move forward, fight for freedom, get out of bad situations or relationships, and accomplish things that seem impossible. Anger can be used as a positive force for personal or collective change – in the beginning of the soul journey.

As we evolve, we reach a point where we become aware of more enlightened ways to respond to life's pain. We realize there's another way to look at things and we're able to slip on the divine lens and see the larger play of light and dark, of awareness and unconsciousness. We begin to understand that every soul here is behaving exactly as nobly as their consciousness allows and appropriately for their stage of soul growth. They're capable of nothing more until they evolve to a higher level of consciousness.

In other words, the murderer is so unconscious and un-evolved spiritually that the inner darkness of their fear-based mind becomes their own personal hell. Only when they ask for wisdom, when they reach out and search for meaning, are they pulled into the light and become capable of living from a state of greater wisdom, awareness and compassion. Until that moment of awakening, the murderer lives in his private hell – even though the outside world does not see or understand this. The murderer gets away with nothing.

Your job as an awakened being is to help awaken consciousness in others – through love and wisdom rather than anger and blame. Your job is to become the beacon of light for those who live in darkness. You must marinate in love and wisdom, surrendering the pitiful ego lens and learning to live mostly within your divine lens. Once this is achieved, you're capable of changing the world, of reforming the murderer – whether he lives inside or outside of you.

Only when we all awaken in consciousness will we be free to live fully in the light of divinity. As long as one soul walks in the darkness, none of us are free. As long as one soul is un-forgiven, we are all un-forgiven.

Today, you may choose to act or think with anger. This is your free will right as a human on Planet Earth. But observe how anger feels in your body. Observe the after-effects of your angry thoughts, words and actions. Then ask yourself; did I change anything or anyone for the better with my anger? Did I help an un-evolved soul wake up? Was I in touch with my soul's wisdom when I acted in anger? Or did it feel like I acted from my lower ego self - fighting with the world for the sake of fighting.

Ask: "What lies beneath this anger I carry towards the world?"

Is it perhaps my deep longing to be back home in the divine realms where we're wrapped in love and light? Am I angry that I'm here and not there? Here and not at home? Have I forgotten that I chose this earthly experience? Have I forgotten that I chose to help others evolve?

Am I angry that there is so much unconsciousness here? How does my anger help bring others into the light? Could sharing my wisdom be more effective in helping others awaken? How different would that feel inside my body? Inside my heart? What would be the after-effects of sharing wisdom to help others rather than relying on old patterns of anger and blame? How might my life change then?

There's a brief moment of silence before we react to someone in anger. Within this brief silent moment lives your choice point. This silence is the gateway to your soul. If you take a deep breath, take an inner step back, and call out for divine guidance, you'll quickly feel yourself lifted out of the reactionary anger of ego, which is the need to attack, defend, justify and blame. Grab hold of that spirit hand reaching down to lift you up and pull you towards the wisdom of divine perspective.

The question is: Do you love the feeling of anger more than you love beauty or grace? Do you understand that by choosing anger you're denying grace and blocking its flow from your own life?

Look at your worthy opponent standing in front of you – the one who sparked your anger. Bless that soul for arriving at this exact moment to show you your next level of inner growth, to give you another chance to pass your soul's test and rise to a higher level of consciousness; a level where beauty, love and grace abounds.

All that's required of you in this moment of anger is to see the other person as a wounded soul doing the best they can from their own level of awareness. Love them for their pain and struggles because you're just like them. By loving them, you're loving yourself. Rise above the unconscious ego behavior they're showing you - because it's ugly, selfish and desperate, and that's not who you are. That's not who you aspire to be.

Look at this lost and pained soul standing before you who has just hurt you, acted from their ego self, and know that you no longer want to look like them, act like them. They're showing you a part of yourself that you're ready to surrender.

One simple breath and a request for guidance, pulls you away from habitual reaction and raises you a notch towards your great soul potential. Thank the messenger for the lesson; thank the soul standing before you who triggered your reaction. Your anger is revealed so that it can be healed.

The next time someone says or does something that triggers your anger, you'll already be removed from the ego experience, more in touch with your soul's wisdom, watching it all unfold from your divine lens. You'll pause, take a breath, adjust your lens, and choose your words gracefully. Compassion will pour through you when you allow it. Quieting the mind and opening the heart is *how* you allow it.

This is the gift of your anger. This is the gift of your opponent arriving with their sword drawn, eager to slice a piece of you. In that moment of sacred recognition, everything changes; you realize that nothing and no one can ever hurt you or tarnish your lovely soul - when you view life through your divine lens.

Jealousy: Courtesy of the Ego Lens

When we view the lives of others through our ego lens, we only see the illusion of who they're pretending to be. We see the illusion of perfection that they've created for protection. We all create this same illusion although some are better at illusion-creation than others.

Every single soul comes here to learn and evolve. If you believe that anyone on earth has it easier or better than you, you're not seeing their soul journey. You're using your ego lens and only seeing the illusion.

We assume we understand who people are when we look at the superficial circumstances of their lives. But we're only looking at their ego story - instead of seeing beyond the surface to understand their soul story. When we wear the ego lens, we can't look deeply enough to see the desperate pain, the tragic losses and the crippling self doubt that lives inside of everyone.

If we did, if we took the time to understand the soul story, to feel the abuse they suffered in childhood, the heart wrenching loss they experienced in early adulthood, or the crippling self doubt they wake up to every morning - we would understand they are the same as us – whether they live in a mansion, a palace, or as a beggar on the street. We're all souls on a journey of evolution having a shared experience here on earth. From this divine perspective, everyone is worthy of your love, compassion and forgiveness.

You may tell yourself that you could be happy if you lived in a mansion or a palace or in a beach house on the ocean; that all you're missing is financial abundance. But this simply means that the lesson you're facing right now is around owning your power through money and career. It's about finding your true work in spite of self-doubt. What you're learning today as you struggle with the lack of money is exactly what you needed to learn in order to evolve to your next level of soul growth.

If you're facing these lessons with anger, bitterness or jealousy then you're not learning what you meant to learn, and you're delaying your own growth.

When you judge a wealthy neighbor or celebrity for their "superficial" lives, you're using your ego lens. You're refusing to see the soul journey and the perfection of each person's journey to consciousness. In your jealousy, you're flunking your soul's lesson and sliding backwards in your own journey to consciousness.

Study the person you're jealous of. Discover their true story. Seek to understand the soul journey. What lessons did they come here to learn? What is their greatest pain? What is their greatest gift? As you dig deeper and truly see what they've experienced in this lifetime, you'll eventually be very glad that their path is not yours. You'll see that their hidden pain and private challenges are not anything you would choose to take on. You'll realize that you prefer the struggles and blessings of your own journey. Then you'll find it easy to offer anyone love, wisdom and compassion.

When you feel jealous, meditate and ask to be lifted from your ego view and shown the soul story of the one you envy. Ask to understand their pain so you can feel compassion rather than jealousy. This will elevate you into divine consciousness and pull you out of your own pain. You're now wearing your divine lens to view the lives of others, and you can check "jealousy" off of your list of soul lessons yet to learn.

(You can also use the numerology and astrology of a person's birth path to help you see them as a soul on a journey. I've described these techniques in previous books and briefly in the workbook at the end of this book.)

From My Soul to Yours: A Day In The Life

I've been having a near-death experience - looking down at this life, bewildered by what I see, confused by how lost we are. I struggle to get my boots back on the ground, assume the position, BE here. I land in the dirt; it hurts my eyes. But I came here on purpose - just like you.

I NEED to see the golden cords tying all of our random and tragic world events together, revealing divine order. I see them sometimes. Not today. Today I feel the weight of fear and despair on my shoulders.

Our crushing human flaw is our focus on the material world and not the spiritual purpose behind it. It is what it is, we say, shrugging our shoulders. This misguided focus repeatedly creates painful spiritual crisis - from which we all will eventually evolve.

Do you tell yourself everyday that you have to work in an industry you dislike, doing work that isn't your mission, just to get your paycheck and benefits? It's what you have to do, you say to yourself - forgetting that this physical world is YOUR dream, YOUR illusion.

Do you tell yourself that your loved one's too early death was a meaningless tragedy from which you don't intend to recover because what's the point? And why feel happy when your loved one is gone?

Do you look around at others to blame for the trivial and tragic moments of your life; everyday traffic (those idiot drivers!), your chronic illness (stupid doctors!), your failing business (the economy is terrible!)?

When your pain gets so great and your life crumbles, do you suddenly cry out for different answers? Do you frantically struggle to clean up your oil spill - the black mess slipping across the waves of your higher consciousness?

Can't we evolve without the crisis? Or does it take a world tragedy to get us to ask different questions, to search for deeper meaning? Can't we live everyday remembering who we are and playing this earthly game from a higher perspective? Will you have to die before you remember who you are? Will WE have to die before we remember that this is a game we came here to play, and that the winners are the ones who live in the love and save everyone else?

You came here to remember your death while still walking on the sands of this shore; To stand in both worlds at once. Impossible? No or we wouldn't have come here.

It's only a simple reaching for your divine lens that's required; a deep breath and a request for guidance that changes everything.

5

SADNESS, DEPRESSION AND ANXIETY: EGO CATARACTS

Sadness comes to you wrapped in illusion. It tells you a tall tale; that you're longing for a loved one on the other side, or a lover who left you, or a career that betrayed you.

But that's never what your sadness truly is. Sadness is a pool, an ocean, a river that sweeps us away when we disconnect from higher self and our soul's wisdom. Sadness and depression are signs that we're living in alignment with ego instead of soul.

A physician will tell you that sadness and depression are nothing but chemical imbalances, to be righted by a drug. And you may try enlightenment through pharmaceuticals. For awhile...

But chemical imbalance is not the source of your sadness. Chemical imbalance is the side-effect of long-term use of the ego lens. Chemical imbalance occurs when the soul disconnects from the higher self. This separation from the soul's wisdom causes your ego mind to dwell on negative thoughts, marinating you in fearful emotions, which then throw your body chemistry into chaos. You become a victim to your negative thought loops -

which you've chosen to indulge in for too many years - or perhaps lifetimes.

You should never discontinue taking prescribed medications unless you're under medical supervision. And I'm certainly not a medical professional. But in my experience with thousands of clients and students, I'm convinced there are effective ways to correct a chemical imbalance other than pharmaceuticals. One of them is by quieting the mind through daily meditation and calling for guidance to help you view life through your divine lens. When we ask for divine guidance we're always answered. This divine intervention helps us break our negative thought cycle.

It's essential to understand the chain of events that create emotional imbalance. It's not simply one incident in our lives that throws us into chronic depression, anxiety, paranoia or schizophrenia. Those diagnoses arrive on the heels of years of making life-style and emotional choices not in alignment with our higher selves.

These choices include everything from poor diets that lack the B-vitamins our nervous systems require, alcohol and drug use that deprive us of our natural chemical balance, and allowing the ego lens to fill us with fear so that we endlessly make choices based on fear rather than trusting the wisdom of our soul.

A mental illness diagnosis is a sign of a deep spiritual and emotional crisis that has been slowly birthed from years of negative, fear-based thinking. We've become disconnected from higher self. To turn this negative cycle around requires reversing all patterns from physical life-style choices to spiritual beliefs. We must recognize our emotional addiction to fear.

Often, by the time a person is diagnosed, they *do* need chemical intervention in the form of prescription medication to break the cycle. But medication is only the beginning of re-aligning with the soul. The person must also take steps on all recovery fronts including nutrition, exercise, vitamin supplementation, counseling to understand the nature of the mind, and spiritual exploration to find greater purpose in life.

(This doesn't have to mean religion or church. It can mean going on a spiritual exploration journey of learning to meditate, taking classes in new thought ideas, and reading books once considered taboo because they were too unconventional or "new age.")

Establishing a personal daily practice of connection to the divine, to something beyond the physical world, is essential for a healthy life. We can meditate, pray, quiet the mind or walk in nature - as we re-establish our connection to highest self.

It's important to understand the true nature of prayer. True prayer is about asking for guidance, wisdom and love – not for things. Many religious followers become disillusioned because they've been taught that God is their Santa Claus in the sky – someone who answers their prayer requests for a new job or car. If that job or car does not appear, they turn away from God and refuse to ever again believe in anything beyond the physical world.

Yet when we pray for "things" we aren't acting in alignment with source and divine order and those prayers are seldom answered. When we ask for light, love and clarity, we're immediately surrounded by divine guides breaking us wide open with wisdom and filling us with love. True prayer is a request for guidance. The ego prays for things. The soul prays for wisdom and courage. The soul is always answered.

Our higher self will caution us against living a life that's not in alignment with our great potential. This guidance shows up as dreams and strong feelings that are nearly impossible to ignore. Our divine lens reveals that living such a life drains us of soul power – also known as energy. The divine lens always reveals the first step that will move us into a life of light, inspiration and love. But *we* must take the step.

Whenever we feel alone, abandoned and afraid, we remember that somewhere, sometime, there was a place that felt differently to us. That felt loving. That felt like home.

Our souls long mightily for this illusive realm, this vague memory where we once lived in light; where our soul mates embraced us and we learned our soul's lessons effortlessly through grace. In this other world that we vaguely recall, we felt completely and absolutely loved in ways that we've only briefly experienced on earth.

Right now, you're standing on this earth because this is the school you agreed to attend. It offers the exact challenges and lessons you agreed to master. It allows your true essence, your unique gifts, to take full form and be fully shared. You volunteered for this experience because you knew it was for your highest good and the highest good of your loved ones.

What could be better or more fulfilling than the evolution of your soul? Once you step onto this path with total surrender, you'll live in divine grace and joyful fulfillment. There's nothing finer, sweeter, richer than this life that awaits you here when you fearlessly embrace it.

Yes, you're desperately homesick for something other, a vague dream, a fading memory of a loving home you once knew. You're hungry for the light, and you pursue it in all the wrong places. But you will be returning to that light soon enough. And when you do, you'll see that this lifetime was a brief opportunity, only the blink of an eye in your soul's journey. You'll understand that this was the lifetime when you intended to let your gifts pour through you to enlighten the world and to banish fear with love.

Your ego cries out: Why am I here all alone in this empty meaningless, unconscious world?

Your soul answers: Because you chose to come here for your highest good and the highest good of all you love. Embrace this moment, seize the opportunity for growth and wisdom, and know that you're never alone.

This earthly realm feels heavy, dense, scary and sometimes dark – especially compared to our memories, our lingering impressions of the higher realms. Depression and sadness are part of our collective human experience in this dense energy. But when we reach for light, call for divine guidance, we're instantly pulled into the light and free of the murky waters of depression and sadness.

Deep sadness has been the marinade of my lifetime. It has washed over me at every challenge, arriving on the heels of each loved one's death, each job loss, each moment of confusion and fear.

I've known sadness as an endless longing. It wrings me out. Only when I find myself broken open, sitting in the mud, tears streaming down my cheeks, do I finally open up, call out for the divine, and ask to be shown the reason for my pain.

In the instant I make that call for inner guidance, send that plea, whisper the words, reach my arms up to the divine, a blanket of loving comfort is wrapped around my shoulders. I'm shown how to get up and move forward.

35

But then I must make the effort to get up. I must make that choice. And in finding my strength to get back up again, I learn the meaning of the lesson and feel the reward of leaning into the pain and stepping into my wisdom.

Sadness and depression are gifts of opportunity. They break us apart until we finally say, "Enough! I'm disgusted with my ego lens and its pitiful view. I will try to view this differently. I'll reach for my divine lens because I truly have nothing left to lose..." In that moment everything changes. We're lifted gracefully into love.

From My Soul to Yours: You never lost anything on that wicked day when you thought you'd lost it all...

The moment you shed your tears, open up, give up, surrender and admit you know nothing - everything gets better. Fast better. Way better. Magic better...

When you wrap your arms around your beloved – the one who won't be coming home again - and you lose your heart, feel it lifting up and away from you, taking wings, leaving like the daylight leaves, you see that nothing here is real. And the person you thought you were is gone - left behind with empty hands.

Later when you've traveled home, stood in your bedroom staring at nothing, you see that the only thing left behind is you - bare naked stripped down to soul - you.

Who is that? How long has it been? How long have you managed the details of your life and forgotten to check on your soul?

That feeling of not knowing who you are now or what matters anymore is your new beginning. It will kick the wind from your stomach, knock you on the floor, and leave you without words – empty. Waiting to be filled with spirit.

One day soon you'll be the just-born baby you once were, bright and shiny with no story attached. No history. No definitions or titles. Just a radiant soul made of energy and love - excited about a new beginning. This is the blessing of your loss.

Throw out your trash. Rip off your clothes. Forget your name, story, bio, and your tragedies. Feel the joy of knowing nothing and being no one. This fresh energy will soar into your newly opened heart like mother's milk. It's what you've needed for a long time. It's necessary to help you realign your great work.

Release each belief you've held so dear, every idea of who you should be, every fear of not being perfect. You've carried this carefully crafted identity, your burden of lies, for too many years. Now the universe has made its own plans for stripping it all away – to help you remember something essential.

That's always the purpose of your loss.

You didn't come here to be someone else or hide behind anyone. You came here to be you – laden with gifts and blessed with challenges. You intended to grow – to push past your fears and expand. You knew coming in that change would be required. When did you forget that?

Look in the mirror and ask 'who am I now?' Is this who I intended to be?

Strip it all away. You never know what lies beneath your tarnished surface until it's all gone. Then you'll see the gold - the beauty of your naked soul. You don't have to figure it all out – to know which steps to take for the next five years. You only need to take the first step. Divine order arranges the rest.

Get out your pencil and erase the spread sheets, delete the to-do lists and the five-year plans, walk into your yard, climb the fence, swim in the lake of your unspoken dreams. Heal yourself.

Turn away from those who remind you of who you've been. Walk out of rooms that keep you small. Take a step into the impossible. This is your new life.

Someday when you've forgotten who you used to be and what you used to want and you believe in things you never would have considered and do things you never would have had the courage to do, you'll catch a glimpse of your beloved – the one who never came home that night – the night your new life began.

You'll see him in the corner of the room, watching you, nodding his head with a smile, sending you the greatest love you ever felt. And you'll know that you never lost anything on that wicked day when you thought you'd lost it all.

The Divine Lens Meditation: Shifting into Soul's Perspective

Practice this technique whenever life feels difficult:
1. Take one deep slow breath – follow it in and out.
2. Mantra or prayer repetition (Om Namah Shivaya) for several moments.
3. Your request: Please help me see my soul's perspective on this challenge.
4. I am grateful for...
5. I open my heart and send love to...
6. This is one positive step I can take today...

Become aware of the importance of physical, emotional and spiritual nutrition on your mental and emotional well-being.

Everything you eat, drink, read, view, think about or pray about affects your mental and emotional health.

To become healthy, you need to embrace physical habits that heal you such as eating fresh, unprocessed, unsweetened foods; rising early in the morning and going to bed before midnight; taking nutritional supplements such as herbs and B-vitamins (under the supervision of a Doctor of Naturopathy); eliminating all alcohol and drugs; reading inspiring and uplifting books; exercising or moving at least 20 minutes per day, and spending time with people who inspire you.

Make a checklist of the daily foods you eat, the beverages you consume, the amount of sleep you get, the amount of time spent in prayer or meditation, the people you're around, and the amount of exercise you get.

Keep track of how these daily activities influence your mental and emotional well-being. When you're ready to heal, you'll have a roadmap of which activities, people and foods serve you best.

See a counselor or therapist who helps you feel positive and optimistic about your future.

6

PERFECTIONISM AND STRESS:
THE EGO'S MACRO LENS

There's no crazy without brilliant; no wisdom without ignorance; no love without hate; and no courage without fear.

Yet we hope to be one without the other – a rose without a thorn. We forget our agreement - to fully experience the light and the dark; to BE human.

We can't own our gifts or our divinity without also owning our pitiful selves and our stupidity; without realizing that our mistakes are what we came here for. They're our greatest moments of awakening.

There's no north without south; no found without lost; no laughter without tears; and no sunrise without sunset.

We come here to feel and express it all; to move through the crazy and find the wisdom; to move through hell and find heaven. Only then can we clearly choose light over dark; love over hate; and wisdom over fear. This is our mission here in the dense realm.

Pretending to be perfect - all good, brilliant, and enlightened is our greatest human flaw. Perfection is our impossible dream here on Planet Earth. How we waste time longing for it, and seeking it in others.

When our beloveds' weaknesses are fully revealed, we stone them, hate them - just as we hate ourselves, for not being perfect, for being ONLY human. We're missing the point of being human; and hurting others with our ignorance.

How eager we are to see another's flaws – to forget that we hold the same flaws in our hands, are made from the same fabric, have spoken the same words, and made the same mistakes. To realize our divine nature is to know that we are all made of this same imperfect fabric.

Create your beautiful life. Sew perfection into every moment. But embrace the defects hidden in your cloth; **know that under the surface, your beautiful life is woven with the same anxieties, fears, hatreds, and mistakes as the life of your greatest enemy. Then you'll realize why there's nothing ever to forgive.**

You'll offer a hand to the one who hurt you most; you'll help them see their gifts and remember their divinity. You'll help them be who they came here to be. Doing this will save you.

The moment you see that your greatest shame, your greatest pain, is also your greatest gift – you'll understand why you're here and who you are.

Love your pain and fear – embrace your darkness. It will lead you to your gifts, your courage and your divinity; it will open your heart. Love the entire story of your imperfect life, especially the grotesque mistakes and ugly self-doubt.

Release your need for perfection in anyone or anything; love the rose along with its thorns. These are the same thorns that live in your heart -alongside the gift of your boundless love.

Become the person who loves the thorn and the gift in everyone – including yourself. Know that one can't exist without the other. Doing this will heal you.

And it will save the life of everyone you meet.

This Imperfection of Perfection

You already know everything. You already know the parts of your story you'll regret. You already know which pieces you'll be proud of. And you already know that your story ends someday.

There is no perfect here. But we long for it like longing for a dream. The impossible perfect lives elsewhere, in another realm, from whence we came. It's the perfection of love, wisdom and spirit. It's higher consciousness.

Our attempts to recreate perfection on earth are often focused on the outer self, the ego, and the details of our material world. We seek to perfect the trivial. Or we demand perfection from others. All of this is misguided.

This world, this realm, is not perfect and never will be. That is not its purpose. You can spend your life on earth expecting perfection from yourself and others, and you will live in constant disappointment and bitterness. You'll lose touch with your soul's wisdom.

Or you can spend your lifetime seeking true perfection - as you once knew it on the other side - perfection of spirit. This is soul alignment. It allows perfect wisdom to flow within you and through you to others.

This type of perfection aligns you with divinity and empowers you to become a source of endless love and wisdom. This is the true perfection that you're seeking after all. Not the false perfection of the physical world that your ego lens focuses upon.

Take an inventory of true perfection in your life. Are you focusing on spiritual growth above all else? Are you asking for divine guidance in your moments of greatest pain? Are you reaching for love and forgiveness when you feel angry and blameful? Are you a channel of divine inspiration in your work? Do you use the unique gifts inside of you to change the world?

If so, you've achieved true soul perfection. This is what you came here to achieve. It's the only perfection you're meant to strive for. Once you achieve this, your life aligns with grace and divine order. You see the light where others see darkness. You know the answers to all questions. You become fearless in adversity. Your heart urges you forward. You accomplish what you came here to do.

If you're caught in the painful trap of false perfectionism, forgive yourself for being misguided, for forgetting what you came here to do. You didn't go through the enormous effort it took your soul to condense itself into a physical body and walk through this dense physical world simply to re-arrange meaningless details.

How do you know they're meaningless? Ask yourself if they will matter to you at the end of your life when you review your lifetime? When you see the ripple effect of each action you performed on earth, each word you spoke, you'll understand then what was essential. You can understand it now.

Where are you seeking perfection today? Do your efforts leave you disappointed, depressed, angry or afraid? If so, you're not seeking divine perfection.

Turn that powerful human drive for perfection towards your inner self, your soul's growth. Seek to have a perfectly loving heart and a sense of inner peace from living in alignment with your higher self. Seek to become a fearless channel to divine wisdom with a career that enlightens the world.

Now your perfectionism is being used for your highest good and the good of others. It's serving its true purpose - correctly focused like a powerful laser on exactly what you came here to do and who you came here to be.

Stress: A Stigmatism of Ego

When we lose touch with the voice of the soul, we feel alone in the world, untethered, shaken, fragile, and overwhelmed by impossible details. We believe that making a mistake will ruin everything. Our creativity is blocked with fear.

This is the distortion of the ego lens. Viewing life through ego lens, we aren't able to see the chords of divine light illuminating our path, or hear inner guidance comforting us. It is this abandonment of higher self that leaves us stunned, beaten down, worried and afraid.

Our ego lens only reveals the trivial details. It obscures the higher purpose, the greater path, the overarching gift of the moment. Through the ego lens, each detail matters equally. Priorities are confused. We cannot move forward.

You are never alone, especially when you feel overwhelmed. Every divine guide who watches over you and each member of your soul family arrives instantly to offer wisdom, to reveal a new idea, to fill you with inspiration, light your way and pull you out of darkness.

Why can't you feel this? You can – by changing lenses. This inner shift begins with the breath. A simple deep inhale and slow exhale begins to align you with spirit, with your soul's wisdom.

Notice how shallow and rapid your breathing is when you feel stressed. When you take a deep slow delicious breath, inhaling fully, exhaling slowly, you begin to move into the light. You infuse your body with divinity. You realign with soul. (This is the real reason why smokers are addicted to cigarettes. It's the only time they breathe deeply. A long inhale on a cigarette changes their energy for the better - until the cigarettes destroy their bodies and thus deplete their energy. Learning deep breathing exercises - without inhaling a cigarette - is very helpful to anyone trying to break this addiction.)

After taking your deep breaths, call out for guidance. Speak your request out loud. Ask for inner clarity and enlightened wisdom. Ask to be pulled out of fear and instead to feel loved and supported and clearly see your next step. Ask for strength and courage. These requests are always answered. These prayers are always heard.

In the moment of prayer, you will suddenly realize you're sitting at a feast - a table laden with nourishment and abundance. But you've been unable to see it. The Ego Lens has blinded you to what's right in front of you.

You're starving - when everything you've ever needed is right in front of you - within reach. You ache with fear when more love than you could ever imagine is already on your plate.

A simple shifting into your divine lens focus reveals the feast of opportunity that awaits you, the abundance of love within reach. It re-organizes priorities. Suddenly you feel as fearless as a hero and as loving as an angel.

7

ADDICTION: EGO LENS SIDE-EFFECTS

When we become addicted to anything or anyone, it's because our ego mind has taken over and drowned out our soul's wisdom. Our ego voice tells us that life is too difficult and physical pleasure is our only relief from suffering in a pointless world. And the ego tells us we need the love of another person to complete us, to feel happy, when we already have a constant divine companion – a higher self and many sacred guides comforting us everyday.

The more we indulge the ego mind and its desires, the more separated from higher self we become. Overuse of alcohol, drugs, sex, shopping, and food steadily replaces prayer. These compulsive behaviors cloud our connection to the higher realms. We've now blocked our access to the sweet nectar of divine wisdom - which flows freely from source and is so infinitely more pleasurable and empowering than physical addictions.

Yet the very act of pursuing drugs, alcohol or any addiction is the act of a hungry soul seeking meaning in an empty world. It's your ego-self crying out for connection to something greater than the physical world. Your ego craves the bliss and love of the divine realms - which you remember vaguely and can briefly recreate in a moment of getting high - before the terrible crash occurs, as it always does, leaving you in a lower, less connected, and more fragile and terrified state than before.

Your addiction is actually your ego's search for spiritual fulfillment, for release from the mundane. It's a cry for relief from the depressing ego lens perspective you've been drowning in. You don't yet realize that you hold within you a divine lens that alleviates the emptiness of the ego mind more profoundly than any compulsive behavior or mind-altering substance ever could.

Your self-destructive act is a cry for salvation - even though you don't realize this and those around you don't realize it either. But your soul understands and waits patiently for you to realign ego with soul, so that all pain can be healed. Your soul sees that you're choosing this lesson as a final step into darkness before you climb into the light permanently. But how far will you fall into that darkness? How long will it take you to crawl out? Will you stay so long that climbing into the light becomes nearly impossible? Only you can decide this.

Within all addictive behaviors exists a brief moment of bliss that is vaguely reminiscent of the higher realms. We feel temporarily comforted. We feel at home, briefly, until the fall from grace - which always arrives on the heels of an addictive act.

Addictive acts are not the pathway back home. They only take us deeper into the abyss where love, wisdom and joy abandon us. There's no greater pain than this abandonment. So we seek more compulsive addictions to alleviate the pain.

Yet the only solution is a shift into higher consciousness - without the aid of a substance or behavior. We're required to make the choice to reach for our divine lens. This will take discipline and courage after we've spent so much time swimming in the muck of unconsciousness. Yet it's possible for everyone. And trying again changes everything.

As humans, it gives us great comfort to know there IS something more to this physical world. Yet if we've reached for that experience through the wrong behaviors our comfort is brief and fleeting. Afterwards, we feel more depleted and depressed than before. Our light dims.

The crash of addiction is a moment of utter terror after the high, when we find ourselves completely submerged in ego and separated from higher self. Our body chemistry is now out of whack and we're fully immersed in fear rather than love. Our behaviors have disconnected us from source, and we no longer embody the higher frequency energy that we need in order to reach out and reconnect.

In this moment, you truly are a lost soul.

Taking a deep breath and calling for guidance will always pull you into the light. But the addict rarely realizes this.

And briefly during a food, drug, or alcohol-induced high – the addict actually does experience something extraordinary; an other-worldly state. He or she accesses a brief moment of divinity. Yet their methods of having this experience defy the laws of the body and leave them more terrified and disconnected than ever before.

The addict has forgotten that they live in a physical body in a physical world with rules for survival. There are sacred laws that must be followed to keep the body filled with life force and the personality aligned with soul. When these rules are violated we suffer from the lower vibration energy we've created within the body. This state is also known as hangover, withdrawal, depression and anxiety.

The ego mind tells us there's no other way to restore balance than to repeat the same unhealthy behavior. But the body chemistry is now out of whack – and it becomes nearly impossible to re-establish a base level of contentment.

The addict has fallen deeply into a hole that is ruled by the ego and ego is now fully in charge - doing its best to block the souls' wisdom. This is also known as "hell."

But the soul is always whispering loving guidance. In brief moments, between bouts of pain, we experience this inner voice of wisdom. Maybe it arrives while we're laid out on the bathroom floor, examining a negative bank balance, or looking in the mirror. In every moment of surrender, the soul speaks up.

If you choose to listen and take a breath, to ask for guidance and seek another way, you'll be lifted into the light, given a new chance, and pulled out of the hole that the ego has dug for you.

This is called spiritual awakening. You can call it a 12-step program, daily meditation, Christianity, Metaphysics, Judaism, Hinduism or Buddhism. It doesn't matter what form it takes.

You're now beginning to embrace your soul's wisdom once again. You're learning to separate from the hell of the ego mind.

Your awakening can cure any addiction. It can heal your broken body. It will mend your broken heart. But it takes work. Inner strength can only be developed in the same way your muscles are strengthened; through disciplined and repetitive use.

If today you suffer from addictions, you're being called to awaken. You're being asked to align with your soul's wisdom and experience the true bliss of higher self. This bliss trumps everything. It's the lesson you came here to learn and the next step of your soul's journey.

Why are we addicted to the ego lens?

There's only one answer to that question: because we're afraid. We're afraid of our own divinity, of our soul's wisdom, of our great potential. If we owned that part of ourselves we wouldn't be able to live small anymore, to dwell in blame, rage, hate and fear. Those easy emotions are powerful and accessible drugs that we sometimes prefer to the effort of reaching for love, wisdom and understanding. These higher frequency emotions require a bit of effort; they ask us to stretch our beliefs, to release old patterns, to ignore the crazy chatter of the world around us, to ignore what others expect of us and instead follow our untested inner wisdom.

If today you struggle with addiction, take these baby steps to help you shift into higher self and out of the pull of ego's desires:

1. **Meditate for 20 minutes to quiet your fear mind.** Use the Sanskrit mantra Om Namah Shivaya (which means I connect to divinity). Don't think about the meaning. Just repeat the Sanskrit phrase and keep redirecting your focus away from your thoughts and back to the sacred phase. Do this twice a day.

2. **Treat your physical body as if you're recovering from an illness:** Eat only live, fresh and raw foods and healthy protein like baked chicken or fish. Drink fresh water all day long – avoiding all sources of sugar and all processed foods. Supplement with B vitamins to boost your nervous system and vitamin C to boost your immune system. Move

at least 20 minutes a day; walk, jog, bike or exercise. Break a sweat at least once day.

3. **Get a spiritual coach/partner to join you on a spiritual exploration journey.** Read and discuss books outside of your comfort zone that stretch your mind with new ideas of how our universe works, who you are and why you're here on earth. Visit a Buddhist or Hindu ashram and spend a weekend in silence and quiet contemplation. Visit a Unity Church and study Course in Miracles. Forgive with abandon. Imagine your life if you truly believed that God is love –pure and simple- and that there is no such thing as a punishing God, or punishing karmas. Imagine that you've landed here in earth school for a temporary journey of spiritual evolution into a life-circumstance that your soul chose as a perfect fertilizer for your inner growth. Consider that you're exactly where you were meant to arrive so that you could wake up today and realize you're here to make a difference in the world, to help others from the wisdom you've learned from your pain; that pursuing this meaningful work and bringing healing to others is the long-lasting bliss and joy you're truly seeking through drugs, alcohol, love, sex or food. Take action on these ideas...

4. **Stay away from toxic friends and situations** that diminish your sense of self and fuel your addiction to ego gratification.

5. **Find an addiction specialist** and follow their recovery program everyday.

8

CYNICISM: 20/20 VISION
OR GLAUCOMA?

When you view life with cynicism, you're wearing your ego lens. Its dark filter is revealing shadows while obscuring light. This is a skewed macro view of the world that focuses on shadowy corners while entirely missing the golden light that infiltrates everything.

You may believe that your cynicism protects you, shields you from ignorance and keeps you from being duped into believing what isn't true. However cynicism is a very low frequency energy and does not serve you, protect you or enlighten you. Cynicism at its core is fear. Fear is the opposite of love. And love is the essence of this divine universe and what we came here to swim in.

Cynicism is the natural state of your left-brain logic mind. It only shows you half of the picture and it blocks the essence of what you need to know. The higher truth, that which is essential, comes from your divine illogical intuitive right brain. It defies logic.

It's the job of your left-brain to filter out everything that lies beyond logic, beyond your five senses, so that you can focus primarily on this physical world to survive, finding food and shelter, and navigating through dense energy.

Yet without your inner guidance, your access to the divine, you're completely lost, unable to see the essence of things or remember who you are. Without your divine perspective, which is free of logic, unbridled, in the creative flow, and immersed in sacred knowledge, you quickly become a lost soul.

Cynicism blocks your inner guidance and your access to the right brain. Cynicism does not exist in your divine lens perspective.

Wearing your divine lens, you understand that everything is evolving for your highest good and the good of all souls. From this perspective, your heart knows that each soul, no matter how they appear on the surface, is behaving exactly as well or terribly as their consciousness allows. You realize clearly that you came to this physical world to help shift consciousness, to shine your love and wisdom on all the lost souls and help them evolve.

Your cynicism only hurts you. It protects you from nothing and no one. It shuts your heart down and disconnects you from divine guidance and flawless intuition. It disconnects you from love.

Cynicism in relationships is a deal breaker – a love destroyer. It brings you into a low vibration frequency where love does not exist. Opening your heart and focusing on the divine essence of another person, seeing them for who they came to be, for their greatness, allows you to help anyone embrace their potential.

Yes you may learn some painful lessons here, just as you agreed to do before you arrived. These lessons are for your highest good and your soul's fulfillment. You may avoid those lessons by stepping over them (using love and wisdom to navigate). But when you live in cynicism, anger and fear you will find yourself painfully slogging through each and every hard lesson you lined up for yourself in this lifetime.

The higher realms are cynicism-free zones. In those realms your heart is wide-open, your love is fierce and unstoppable, and your essence is trusting. You embrace wisdom above all else.

Name it what it truly is: cynicism is fear. Nothing more. Nothing less. When you live in the murky waters of fear, you suffer. You fall far from grace. You swim amongst the sharks. You plummet into the hell realm rather than swimming in the sweet ethers of divine love.

Cynicism does not protect you. To be protected, you need clear access to your divine intuition. Your soul reveals truth to you 24/7. You may be used to shutting this voice out, this divine whisper, but your inner wisdom (which comes from the heart and speaks in the voice of love) is the key to your success and happiness on earth. This wisdom tells you where to take your next step, whom to love, and what career to embrace.

Your cynical mind pushes you into doubt where you live in a world of evil-doers, tragic events, meaningless work, and futile effort. Nothing you do is ever good enough. Nothing anyone does for you is ever good enough. People are selfish and out to get you, according to the cynical mind. You must be on guard because evil is more powerful than you are - says the ego.

This is ALL true when you're not hooked up to your soul's wisdom and divine intuition.

Cynicism attracts lower frequency experiences and less evolved souls. Cynicism attracts empty jobs, meaningless work, and futile effort. Everywhere you look, you see the harshest lessons, the cruelest acts, the unkindest people. And you have now become one of them. You have become what you feared most. And your fearful energy contributes to the darkness.

The world as a whole is more cynical today than ever. This is because the overall vibrational speed of the energy on our planet has increased. As the vibration increases, our growth accelerates. As with all change, resistance is mounted equal to the gathering momentum for expansion. We're at a tipping point for fear vs love and cynicism vs consciousness.

Which side are you on? What is your prevalent viewpoint? Are you a cynic? Do you find all kinds of logical reasons to embrace this viewpoint and wear this lens?

Yes there are many corrupt people in positions of power on our planet. This has always been true for as long as life has existed on Earth. Those who have much to learn ascend quickly to power partly because of their unconsciousness, their inability to see the essence of things and remember their soul's mission. This gives them a kind of fearlessness and ruthlessness required to gain power in a low-consciousness political system.

These unconscious and greedy people are frequently in the spotlight. We're fascinated by them for a reason. Watching their inevitable downfall enlightens us. Our soul is taking notes.

Yet view it this way: As each soul is brought into media scrutiny its inner growth is spurred. This is a byproduct of the enormous attention humans receive in the public eye. This energy accelerates their vibration until they come face to face with their greatest soul lessons - which then unfold before us.

Any intense focus on a person's life serves as a soul catalyst – though you may not always see this growth unfolding from your television screen. The seeds of growth are within all of us, and the hot lights of media burst these seeds into life.

There are infinitely more awakened and conscious beings living on this planet than non-awakened beings. You are one of these awakening ones, working behind the scenes to shift us into the light.

Divine consciousness is ultimately more powerful than the unenlightened acts of unconscious souls. The spiritual teachers, healers, writers and artists amongst us are the ones holding the light - even if these individuals appear less famous or less successful than the un-awakened. All lessons are learned in the end. Light trumps the darkness every time.

Choose your side...

9

SOUL STORIES

These Soul Stories scattered throughout the book are based loosely on the lives of clients I've worked with and are designed to help you understand how using your divine lens determines the choices you make and thus the direction of your life.

Marie: Light and Color

Marie grew up in Minnesota as the oldest of three kids in a poor farming family. When she was six years old, her mother was diagnosed with breast cancer. For the next two years she helped take care of her dying mother, dress, feed, bathe and care for her two younger siblings and fill in for a dad who, after a night of hard drinking, packed his bags and left without a forwarding address.

When Marie was 9, her mother died and she was sent to live with an aunt, followed by another aunt, and eventually put into foster care. Her younger brother and sister were scattered in the foster care system and her sister died of pneumonia shortly after. These years were tough for Marie but she held out hope of seeing her brother again someday. She stayed strong for him.

Marie says she always knew she was guided somehow. From an early age she was aware of light even in her darkest moments. She knew in her heart that her mother would die from the day she heard the diagnosis, yet she also knew that she would be okay, taken care of. She didn't understand how or why she felt this way, but she trusted her feelings. They'd always served her.

She was only brought into a church a few times in her youth, and she didn't really understand religion. But she sensed a bigger world around her, something unseen and peaceful that she could tap into in her quiet moments, even in the midst of caring for a dying mother or adjusting to a strange foster home. She intuitively knew that her Divine Lens perspective – accessed easily whenever she colored or painted – was her ticket to a better life. Her inner world was filled with vivid color and light. So she spent her extra time pursuing art; coloring, drawing or water painting whenever she could find the art supplies to do so.

Even as a young child, she seemed to know or sense whom to gravitate towards and whom to avoid. She was drawn to adults and kids with a certain quality about them, an inner light, or a voice that seemed more wise and kind than others. She navigated with this sense of moving towards light, avoiding darkness. And it served her well in the various foster homes where she grew up. Excelling in school and in art brought her happiness and a sense of meaning in spite of her living situation.

In high school, she longed to do something significant with her life. She longed to help kids who were lost and untethered like she had been. As a child, she had taken care of her younger siblings and her heart ached for them terribly. Helping other young children would ease this pain, she believed.

When a high school teacher suggested she apply to a University of Minnesota education program to become a teacher she knew it felt like a good first step. She applied for and received a fully paid scholarship to college.

In college, her passions evolved into education and counseling, so she double majored in education and psychology. After teaching in a public school for two years, she became restless with the system and applied for a grant to attend graduate school in psychology with an emphasis on school counseling. She loved every minute of grad school and graduated with honors. She quickly found a new job as a school counselor.

At first she loved counseling kids in the school system, but during the Saturn Returning reinvention point of her late twenties, she longed for something more. She wanted to inspire kids by helping them tap into their creativity, to embrace the arts as she had done as a child. Art had brought such comfort during her childhood traumas, and she wanted to help children find their inner healing through color and light as she had done. She returned to school for an art education degree and reinvented her career to be an art teacher.

She became the teacher everyone loved. Her room was filled with color and her teaching style inspired students to find the artist within, to use light as their navigating principle.

She married just as she turned 30, and raised two kids; a girl named Faith and a boy named Lark. Raising her children was the most healing experience she'd ever known. She realized she was healing her childhood pain by becoming the mother she never had.

When her son Lark was 17, he was killed by a drunk driver in a car accident. Marie was devastated, unable to get out of bed for days. In a dream, her son came to her and told her to get up, to keep going, that he loved her, watched over her and that all was well. He told her he was happy and wanted her to be happy.

But she still struggled with terrible grief. When she went back to work, she poured her heart into helping her students more than ever before. Each time she saw a student suddenly believe in himself, take a risk and gain confidence, she felt a little more healed herself.

Her husband couldn't face the pain of losing their son. He drank himself to bed most nights and his energy cast a pall over the house. Marie knew that the light and color she needed to live in was gone from the house, and that either her husband had to wake up and live again, or she had to leave him. After many long talks, counseling sessions, and many tears, Marie moved out. It was the hardest thing she'd ever done. Now she was grief stricken and divorced.

Her grown daughter was now her best friend, and they comforted each other greatly. At first they shared an apartment to keep expenses down and for the companionship they both needed.

Marie's work with children kept pulling her forward, lighting up her soul. A couple years later, the thought occurred to her that she wanted to help grieving children heal by connecting them to art, color and light. She found a program in art therapy and received financial aid and a small grant.

After a couple years of part time grad school while continuing her teaching job, she graduated as a certified art therapist. At the end of the school year, she announced her plans to open a private art therapy practice, and slowly began seeing clients. Her specialty was helping those who grieved find their way back to life - through color and creativity.

Her work was so inspired and heartfelt that her practice grew rapidly. Her clients said that being in her healing presence was a blessing for them, and that the work they did together was life-changing. And Marie loved her clients. Their stories of grief and loss inspired her. With each client she helped, Marie felt more healed herself.

Marie's divine lens grew stronger with each new phase of her life, with each new choice made for love and light. She had learned to approach everyone with love, to bring color and light into every room, to help every client who came to her to shine in their own possibilities and to blossom into their gifts.

She attracted many adult clients including a man who'd lost his wife to cancer. He fell in love with Marie's inspiring approach to life, her gift of healing, her deep inner sensitivity and spiritual wisdom.

They married and navigated the challenges of combining households. Her grown daughter was thrilled about the marriage but his teen-aged kids, still grieving their mother, were slow to accept Marie into their life. But with love and time, they did. Marie felt that her presence in their lives helped them heal while they also helped her heal the loss of her son.

As she continued to help her clients navigate challenges, she remembered her own pivotal moments of choice, many of them early in her lifetime, when she had faced a fork in the road, a choice to focus on the dark side of humanity or to focus on the light and goodness she could find everywhere.

She remembered how she'd struggled at first when her mom got sick as she cared for her siblings while she was herself still a child. And she remembered the terror of foster care and how, with each new challenge, the choices got easier because the pattern was being established that she would choose love over fear.

As Marie grew older, and heard from the children she'd once taught or counseled, she realized that helping children had spilled over into many other lives and impacted so many people positively. And she discovered that her ex-husband had grown and evolved because of how lovingly she'd offered him choices to heal, and how clear she had been in choosing her own life, rather than living in his darkness. This made her happy.

Her courage and love, it seemed, had spread like fire, awakening and empowering many others. For this, she was and still is beyond grateful. She continues to see clients as an art therapist.

10

Part One Homework:

Shifting from Ego Lens to Divine Lens

1. To Determine Which Lens You're Wearing Today:

Ask yourself:

How do I feel in my body? Tense, relaxed, energized or depleted?

Am I feeling love towards anyone, everyone, myself?

Am I feeling compassion towards my opponent?

Do I feel that all is well in the world or does life feel tragic?

Am I feeling afraid or confident?

Do I feel insecure or inadequate in any area of my life?

Do I feel judged by others or judgmental towards others?

Do I feel sad and heavy with grief?

Do I feel passionate about my work?

Do I feel exhausted and depressed?

Do I feel joyful and grateful?

Answering these questions will let you know which lens you're wearing today.

Feeling tense or depleted physically, afraid, insecure, sad, depressed, shut down, or angry is a sign of divine lens deficiency. It's time for a new prescription.

Your Powerful Lens Shifting Prescription:

1. Imagine you've just had an interaction with someone who has angered or hurt you. Feel that familiar triggered self-defense reaction.
2. Take a deep long inhale and exhale while focusing only on your breath.
3. For extra credit or to help quiet the ego mind, repeat a Sanskrit mantra such as Om Namah Shivaya for several minutes – keeping your mental focus only on the words of the mantra – rather than your thoughts.
4. When you feel your mind settling down, say: Please show me the wisdom of this moment and reveal how my soul sees this challenge – not my ego. Help me to hear my soul's wisdom and quiet the chatter of my ego mind.
5. Get a notebook and pen and begin writing: My soul says that the lesson of this moment is....
6. After you've written on that question for a while, begin writing this: My action step to solve this problem for everyone's highest good is...
7. Write quickly so that the words flow from your right brain higher consciousness and not from your logical left-brain monkey mind which is where your ego chatter lives.

These three steps will help you shift into your divine lens today:

1. **Focus on one thing in your life you can feel grateful for right now.** Keep focusing on it as if you are wearing binoculars and exploring it up close. See each detail of what you're grateful for. Now open your heart and send that one object or person you're grateful for a big burst of love. Wrap them in compassion. You've now shifted into your divine lens. Focus your divine lens on the challenge you're currently facing, and send compassion to the people who are troubling you.

2. **Take a deep breath with a long inhale and long exhale.** Say: Please divine guides show me the lesson of this moment and reveal the divine lens view of this story I'm telling myself today. Pull me out of the ego view and show me the wisdom of this lesson. Write your thoughts on this:

3. **When I look back at this difficult moment in my life how will I think of it?** How will I wish I had handled this challenge from my most enlightened compassionate perspective? Looking back at this moment in your life, describe your soul story of how you gracefully overcame this challenge by choosing love over fear:

Ask yourself these questions:

1. What is the purpose of my life – other than financial survival? How can I change my career to more fully align with this more meaningful pursuit? What baby steps can I take this month?

2. Why would my soul (choosing circumstances for my highest good and never out of punishment) have chosen to come here and experience the life I've lived?

3. What gifts may have been hidden in my moments of greatest pain? These are gifts of awakening that I can only realize now as I review my past painful moments:

4. What does my greatest self know to be true about using my gifts and talents to make a difference in the world?

5. What steps would I take to begin doing that now to make my living?

6. What changes would I need to make in my life and in my relationships to move forward?

PART TWO:
THE GIFT OF YOUR DIVINE LENS

I pray to be brought into alignment with the wisdom of highest self. I pray to align with the light and separate from ego self so that divinity inspires all my words and actions.

From My Soul to Yours:

There's a Journey You Have to Take

There's a journey you have to take – a paddle to shore – a trip through your shark-infested mind. It's your journey from dark to light – from fear to love – from nowhere to everywhere.

Reach down now and dip your hand into those dark swirling waters. Start a ripple. Make a stir. Embrace the danger and adrenalin blending inside of you. That's the energy of your pure life force waking up. It's YOU moving from lost at sea to found again.

Dip in with your hand now - palm facing behind you. Wave away what's done and gone. You will move forward. Pain is part of this ride. You knew that going in. Let divine grace push you into the current now. Surrender. You'll find your new posse on the shore. You'll find your good work once you let go.

This ride to shore could last a lifetime. You may forget to breathe. There will be terrible storms along the way. You'll cry while you paddle. And there will be days when the sea is calm and the sky glorious and nothing else matters. You will get lost.

But soon you'll see your loved ones standing on the shore in the glow of sunlight beckoning to you. You'll wave your arms and shout with joy. And you'll remember something long forgotten.

Once you're ashore, you won't understand what held you back. Nothing. Nothing ever held you back. Maybe you forgot to breathe. Maybe you cried. But nothing ever stood in your way.

Perched on your board now, sitting in the deep-water channel, you won't want to move. Shore will look so far away. Beyond hopeless. Your arms will ache in anticipation. You'll see the impossible journey ahead and reject it before you begin.

I'm not strong enough, smart enough, good enough to do this, you'll whisper to the wind. You may even turn your board around to face the wide open sea with its unknown pleasures, invisible islands beckoning with promises of salvation. But taking that course will only lead you into a bigger storm and a longer paddle to shore through shark infested waters.

Yes, the sharks will circle. But they're afraid of your strength. They feed on fear. When you fight back you survive. When you quit paddling, fear will feast on your heart. And your heart is your lifejacket, your one good surfboard to freedom, your only hope.

Lift your gaze from their dark fins. See the moon above you like a gem in the night. Kiss that blessed moon. Reach up and wave your arms like the symphony conductor you came here to be. Move the stars with your grief and craft them into your personal sonata. This midnight song from the depths of your heartbreak will be the masterpiece of your life.

When the sun begins to rise you'll find more strength. You'll push harder against the waves. You'll move forward in leaps. But nothing happens until you dip in. Dip your hand into the dark scary water. It will save you.

Dip in. Dip in now. Take one stroke with your aching arms. Move forward one inch. One inch is everything. One stroke is your entire world. One more stroke is your entire future. A current will catch you. It's always something you didn't expect. Didn't believe in. That suddenly moves you forward.

You'll find yourself gliding effortlessly now. You'll sit back for a moment and breathe. You'll scan the vast horizon in front of you. It looks closer than you thought. Anything is possible, you'll whisper - even if you don't truly believe it.

Now you're beginning to feel strong. You'll dip into the dark water over and over. No longer afraid. Focused only on the shore. You understand now. You see the journey for what it is – a brief ride to shore that requires everything you have and makes you strong. It pulls you into light – the light you've always longed for but didn't know what you were missing. Didn't know where your homesickness came from. Your deep sorrow. Your endless longing. It was all for this.

This IS the journey home. It's the only journey to take. It's underneath you and in front of you. Dip in my friend. There's nowhere else to go. These swirling waters will soon turn into grateful tears. Those last yards to the shore are shallow and clear. You see the beauty of each life with each stroke you take.

When you come ashore, you'll fall into the arms of your beloveds. There will be bonfires and dancing barefoot in the sweet sand. Your lovers from past, present and future will hold you. They'll whisper tender words. The ones who once broke your heart completely will now hold you tightly while you cry.

You'll share stories around the fire. These will be the greatest stories you've ever heard or ever told. It will all make sense – the shark-infested waters, the nights of dark despair and the endless longing.

You will find this shore without a compass, without a lover, without a mother, you'll find your way. You'll find it because you once dipped your trembling hand into the dark water and shoved yourself forward into the storm.

You can lie down then laughing on the beach - looking up into the eyes of your beloveds. Running the soft sand through your fingers. "Were there really sharks?" You'll ask. And you'll laugh out loud at the sound of your words.

When you find your people standing in a circle around you – the ones you thought you'd never see again and the ones you weren't sure even existed – your heart will break wide open, shattering into a million tiny pieces of light – like diamonds on the open waves guiding someone else to shore.

II

Seeing Death as Transformation

It's the morning of July 14, 1980. I awaken to the sounds of a mourning dove outside my window and a view of Boulder's sacred limestone slabs reaching into the clouds; these front range Rocky Mountain slopes are where my husband and I once spent happy afternoons climbing, hiking and feeling invincible.

Yesterday, this elegant and strong young man died from cancer at the age of 34. His death ended a year of unforgettable suffering for both of us. My ego tells me this is a deplorable soul-sucking tragedy. Paul was the most loving man I'd ever known and did not deserve to suffer and die before his life could unfold – before we could have our future.

No one will ever love me like that again, says the ego mind. I'm alone, grief-stricken, and sick with heartbreak. I'm scarred for life - just as he was at the end. But I'm still here and he is not.

This voice in my head crushes and flattens me, pushes me back into bed, feels like molten lead pouring down. It deletes my future. I feel miniscule underneath these heavy thoughts. "Why would my husband die of cancer when everyone else our age is launching careers and having babies? What kind of loser am I?" whispers the ego.

Hours later and with tremendous effort, I push out of bed and step outside on the balcony, gazing up at the jagged pink flatirons jutting into a cloudless sky. I take a deep breath and observe their beauty, remember their promise.

It stirs a memory of a time when I first chose Boulder, chose to come to Colorado from the flatlands, with no money or job, just courage and determination. I wanted to break away from old fear patterns, to climb these dizzy rocks even though they terrified me. Magical things happened when I got here; an impossible mountain climbing career, marvelous friends, soul-mate-love and unprecedented happiness.

This reminiscence stirs a powerful recognition inside of me. I've chosen the path of courage before. And it served me well.

The voice of inner wisdom that has been knocked out of me for the past year, now whispers: This is your greatest moment. Every lesson you came to learn in order to push into your soul's potential and align with your highest self, lives in this very instant of devastating grief.

The energy of these words lights me up, gives me breath. My mind chatter quiets and I hear my higher self say: Paul was your greatest spiritual teacher. He revealed his spirit to you as he left his body. He took you on a spiritual journey disguised as a healing journey. It was your healing journey, not his. It was his gift to you.

Over the next few months, I begin to realize that all the things we experienced together in the year of his dying - the meditations, healers, Native American ceremonies, and his fully conscious exit from his body - were all for me. He was finished with this lifetime, not meant to stay longer, just long enough to show me that I was worthy of love and could reach into my soul to find wisdom and courage. He helped me see life in a new way.

"You've never been alone," whispers this inner voice of the divine. "You've been held in love and light even in your darkest moment. You must choose which path to take now. This is your choice point."

The next few years of my life play out as up and down as a roller coaster. Sometimes I'm able to embrace my divine lens view and move forward. Other times I'm lost in self-pity, self-doubt and the blind confusion of anger and grief.

Along the way, I battle fear, bankruptcy, heartbreak, self-doubt, anger and loneliness. Yet my choice will ultimately be for trusting my soul's wisdom and consciously taking the spiritual path that gets me here - writing this to you.

Our journeys are never one straight line of uninterrupted wisdom and enlightened action. Neither are they one continuous journey of negativity and fear. All of us vacillate between our ego lens and divine lens perspectives. We spend time viewing life through each lens so that we can make a fully realized choice. These two viewpoints battle for dominance inside of us until our heart finally chooses. This choice becomes the essence of who we are.

This is the point of human evolution. Before we arrive, we're immersed in the divine realms where the light is vivid and vibrates with love and our heart connections are deeply satisfying. We simply wouldn't be drawn to choose fear and darkness over love and light while existing in that sacred dimension. Yet our consciousness needs to expand; that's the nature of consciousness and energy. We created this earth school, this dense energy realm, for the sole purpose of consciousness expansion - for all of us.

Our collective consciousness chose to push down into this earth energy so that, ultimately, we'd be able to dwell simultaneously within all levels - from this luscious and sensual physical realm to the highest realms of light. There would be no death. We'd eliminate the veil between realms. Our collective souls would be pushed to new levels of awareness, love and light. We would add a rich dimension to our existence as souls – this physical realm.

You were born here with that intention. Billions of years ago, the energy was denser on earth, less light-filled. Our souls were still learning the basics of survival in a physical world. Our journeys to this realm were shorter with briefer life spans.

Jesus, Buddha and numerous other teachers courageously incarnated here to expand our levels of consciousness to extraordinary new heights, merging light with dark, teaching love over fear, waking us up from the unconsciousness we'd dwelt in here on earth for so long.

As we collectively work on this evolution, more light is penetrating this dense realm. We've gradually all become more conscious while here on earth.

Today we stand at a pivotal moment in this awakening. It will take all of us to push the final mantle of fear and darkness away. Eventually we'll all make a final choice for the divine; for love over fear and light over dark.

As impossible as it may feel sometimes, you're one of the consciousness shifters here. Or you wouldn't be reading this. You wouldn't be aware enough to ask meaningful questions, to realize that you were once lost in fear and don't intend to live that way again. You wouldn't know there was a divine lens perspective unless you'd already shifted out of ego lens.

Now you're awakening and bringing others with you. You stand on the precipice of conquering ego, fear and darkness. You're being lifted into the light at this very moment.

Take a breath, silent your mind, and listen. Push away any thoughts that frighten you because they're not real. Breathe in the life that you came here to know; a life of love, courage and light. This is your moment.

If grief is your greatest teacher, if right now you stand on the precipice of shattering loss, you are blessed.

Your loved one, now on the other side, is trying to help you remember who you are and why you stand here on earth. It only takes silence and listening to know that your departed lives on.

Yes you'll have to battle the ego mind telling you that life is meaningless and you will never love again. Listen to that song of woe and fear that the ego mind plays. How does it feel in your body?

Does it suck your life away, drain your energy, keep you in bed? Does it sit on top of you like molten lead crushing your soul? That is the job of the ego self, to bury us in unconsciousness.

Yet at this very moment, your divine self is also speaking. It speaks with love and fearlessness. The very sound of its words stir energy within you, lift weight from your shoulders, fill you with breath and light, with inspiration.

Your higher self says: this is the greatest moment of your lifetime! All the lessons you came to learn live in this moment of transformation. See the beauty of every miss-step and every soul agreement that has brought you here. See the perfection in all of it. Choose the light. Choose the love. The rest will unfold as it should.

Let Me Tell You a Story...

In April of 2015, my husband Gene drove us up Four Mile Canyon to the little Chapel of the Pines where my first husband Paul and I were married in 1979. So many memories flooded back to me of that happy sunny September day filled with love and hope.

As we drove down the canyon we saw the little cabin beside the creek where Paul and I first lived and had our sweet wedding reception. Both places miraculously survived flood and fire and are impossibly still standing.

Think Paul must have watched over them...

It brought back so many powerful sensory memories to be there. I sat on the chapel steps and cried for 20 minutes. I remembered how happy my dad was that day and how much he loved Paul, our wedding, and our cabin. **Dad and Paul are both watching out for me now from the other side.**

Sitting on those steps I felt my dad, Paul, Crissie and Marv all with me. In the hard years following that amazing wedding day in 1979, I lost all of them to cancer - except for Marv who died of a stroke at the age of 44. **Yet I'm grateful for the heartbreak I experienced then which sent me on my spiritual journey.**

Today I have my incredible husband Gene Malowany and our miraculous children Sarah and Kai - and my amazing career - none of which I would have without going through my journey.

Gene sat beside me today listening to my memories and soaking up the experience. He understands everything about my life and where it's brought me. It was his idea to drive up there. I hadn't been up that canyon since 1980. I was grumpy on the drive up finding a million reasons not to go - some part of me realizing what I'd remember as soon as I saw that sacred place.

Yet once I released the flood of emotion that rose up in me... I saw with great clarity the gift of my life story and the gift of loving so many amazing souls along the way.

Facing Death With Grace

When we're diagnosed with a terminal illness it's an extraordinary opportunity to see each day through the divine lens. This is our most empowering perspective when facing death. It's where we find courage to face the unknown.

Our ego view of the world is shattered daily through illness. As the body deteriorates, we learn that the ego mind is not in charge; that it only reveals part of the picture, and that fear is our greatest enemy.

Many souls choose the transformational grace of the path of terminal illness to shatter the ego, release negative patterns, and shift fully into the soul's perspective, the divine lens view.

If you've chosen this path of awakening, in your final days you'll experience visitations and dreams from departed loved ones - even as your left-brain logic mind tries to deny it.

You'll slowly be pulled into expanded consciousness while you're still living in the body. This can be an extraordinary awakening for anyone especially those who've lived life unconsciously – tethered to the ego.

If you've been diagnosed with a serious illness, ask yourself: Are you sensing things differently? Are your perceptions expanding? Do you long to talk about death but you're afraid to upset those who love you and want you to live? This is all part of the process of returning to the higher realms.

You'll find it comforting to retell the story of your life to a loved one. This is a good place to start the journey of releasing your memories and attachments. As you review your life story, consider this: What were you learning in your most painful moments? What were the gifts from your pain? What are you grateful for now? What moments of grace and divine intervention do you see today that you couldn't see then?

If you retell your story the old way - through ego lens perspective – your higher self will cause interference, create static to disrupt your outlook. You'll experience moments of profound and surprising wisdom as your soul reveals past hardships through a more enlightened point of view. Unresolved feelings and regrets will surface for review. Forgiveness is beginning to illuminate your memories. This is your pre-departure soul review.

It gives you another chance to open your heart before the lifetime concludes.

Meditate for a few minutes each day, sitting quietly, eyes closed, repeating a sacred mantra or prayer, and you'll experience openings in your awareness. As you get closer to death, you may have precognitive visions of future events that will unfold for your loved ones after you're gone. These can include divorces, weddings, births and losses. Use your precognitive awareness to initiate healing conversations. Bring wisdom and compassion to these discussions to help your loved ones face an uncertain future without you.

Past hurts will resurface into your consciousness for healing. You'll long to communicate with and forgive those you discontinued friendship with long ago. This is your soul giving you an opportunity to see things as they are - rather than as your ego lens has distorted them.

Allow this process of surrender to unfold gracefully. Your soul wants to you finish this lifetime well; to accomplish the awakenings you came to experience. The more you quiet the mind through meditation or prayer, the better you'll use this sacred time for what it's intended to be – an opening to higher self.

When you're afraid of what's coming, meditate to quiet the mind. Ask your guides or your higher self to reveal what happens when you die. Ask to visit the divine realms in your dreams.

Keep a journal. Writing will help you open your channel to the divine. Write this sentence at the top of a page: This is the graceful exit I'll experience as my soul is set free from the body and I ascend to the realm of love and light.

Write that phrase several times and keep writing. Describe the graceful exit you're about to make. Let the words flow through you. Write quickly. Let your pen move freely and don't edit or review what you've written. Writing quickly without over-thinking allows you to bypass your logic brain and download guidance directly from your highest self. Wisdom will channel through your words.

Try this writing exercise often until you're aware of the difference between words that come from your left-brain critic and words that flow from a source greater than your mind. When you embrace the wisdom from beyond your mind, your writing will calm your fears of death.

In your final weeks and days on earth, allow the essence of love to fill your heart. As you surrender to the process, you'll be pulled gracefully into the bliss of transformation from this world to the divine.

Death is an act of love. It's a surrender into greater love than you've known on earth. Allow this. Your guides are here to help you. The moment you take your final breath, you're set free of the dense body. Your spirit returns to the happy, loving essence of you. This is how you began this lifetime and how you'll end it.

You may be greeted by departed loved ones. And you may be pulled to visit your loved ones on earth as they learn about your death. You'll comfort them in their moment of grief. Some of them will respond to your presence and others won't seem aware of your visit. When it's time, a divine being will guide you towards the light of the highest realms.

You'll be shown the soul's perspective of your life here on earth. You'll see objectively, in a non-judgmental way, the soul lessons you came to learn and the great gifts you brought with you. You'll see and feel the ripple effects of your actions towards others. You'll be shown the choices you could have made but didn't.

You'll feel the pain you caused others as well as the love that your positive actions and words created. This instantaneous, non-linear viewing of your life story detaches you from ego and aligns you fully with soul.

As you finish the life review, you'll be shown into another level of the highest realms where you'll meet teachers who reveal more about the purpose of your journey to earth. They'll review your soul's progress compassionately.

You'll continually be drawn back to earth to comfort grieving loved ones. Since time is not linear, you'll feel them call you, and you'll wrap them in healing love even as you ascend to higher levels of consciousness.

Helping Someone You Love Face Death

Releasing our loved ones to the divine realms without anger or sadness is one of the hardest tasks we face on earth. The only way to accomplish this is by viewing death through the divine lens perspective.

Your ego mind will tell you that losing your loved one is a tragedy and that you're a victim to cruel circumstances. The ego will weigh you down with sadness, depression and grief - long before your loved one actually departs. These negative feelings will hamper your ability to open your heart and love fully in their final days. You'll miss a great opportunity for tenderness, forgiveness and gratitude.

This simple prayer request will help you open your heart and surrender to the process of letting go: Show me the soul's perspective on my loved one's death. Reveal to me how I can best help them.

From this enlightened perspective, you'll understand the soul agreement you made with your loved one long before this lifetime began. You'll remember that you agreed to release them with love and courage, and to remain here for **your** soul's growth and evolution. Fulfilling this agreement requires all of your inner strength, but that's exactly why you agreed to it. Inner strength is exactly what you needed to develop within yourself.

You also agreed to stay here in order to fulfill your greatest work - which is still unborn within you. This painful lesson is a huge gift to you from your beloved; it's the gift of pain that you can transform into fuel to do your greatest work.

Surrender to the grace of your pain, and release your loved one with wisdom and strength. Tell your dying beloved that you'll be fine without them. This helps them release the body.

Say: I love you and will love you forever. Tell me how I can help you depart with grace? Tell me how I can help you release this lifetime. Tell me how I can serve you best?

Whether your beloved is conscious or not, sit beside them and share memories. Discuss their childhood and reminisce over good times. If they're conscious, ask open-ended questions about their moments of greatest pain and challenge.

Ask them who they'd like you to contact from their past. Ask what they learned from their hardships. Ask how they want to be remembered. These loving questions get them started on the process of surrender.

Discuss their beliefs about where they're going. Ask how they feel as they approach death. Casually discuss differing spiritual viewpoints about afterlife - even if these aren't the ideas they grew up believing. You might say: "What do you think of the Buddhist idea of reincarnation? Do you believe there's a hell? Do you believe you'll see departed loved ones?" Explore spirituality through books, conversations, movies, meditations and prayer. This will help them find peace.

You'll know when it's time to directly ask: "How can I help you face death?" Listen to everything they say and follow their lead. Everyone dies in their own unique way – which is similar to how they lived.

If your loved one has always been a private person, they may want to die alone. If they love being with others, they'll probably want to be surrounded by friends and family in their final hours. If they ask to die in your arms, they'll wait until you're holding them to release the body. The soul, not the conscious mind, chooses the final breath.

If you release your loved one with grace and wisdom, no matter how devastated you feel, you'll be giving them a magnificent gift. Your loving release is an act of total surrender for another's highest good. By doing this gracefully, you may also be accomplishing your most important task of the lifetime.

Let me tell you a story...

A big part of me just wanted to run out crying into the night, to stand under the stars, to look at beauty instead of pain.

Last night I spent two hours having a "what happens when we die" conversation with a friend I've known since the 80s. She's 50 years old and dying from stage four cancer. It was diagnosed three months ago.

She said her friends don't talk to her about spirituality and crossing over. She's been an atheist much of her life - although she's done amazing work for the world in her career.

She had my book Bridges to Heaven: True Stories of Loved Ones on the Other Side - on her nightstand. She asked me to sit with her to talk about it.

She said she'd spent her life not wanting to believe in that kind of "woo-woo" stuff. But now she was having experiences that she believed were some kind of inexplicable divine order and wanted to explore ideas she'd not been comfortable with before.

She cried for most of the two hours during our talk - releasing so much fear and grief she's been holding on to. She's devastatingly frail and in constant pain. She lives alone. Hospice visits twice a day. It was so hard to see her suffering and so afraid of death.

I taught her to meditate - as well as some other sacred techniques for releasing fear - like my Break Your Heart Wide Open meditation. I gave her a rosewood Mala - which she loved.

She was so grateful I'd visited and will try to meditate now when's she's alone and afraid. She wants me to come back. And I will...

But it was so hard to be there. I'm so inadequate in those situations. The visit brought back so many memories of my husband Paul, best girlfriend Crissie, and my dad who all died too young - from cancer.

Afterwards, my husband Gene and I talked about my visit. It helped so much to talk to him and feel his love and support. Our views on life and death are fully aligned and I'm so grateful for him.

But today I can't get the images and smells of the visit out of my head. All I want to do is go shopping and buy some expensive Eileen Fisher clothes that I can't afford. I know that's just my grief acting up. It's my old relentless question of why do good people often take the path of suffering before they die? That one painful question launched my spiritual exploration journey in the 80s. And it still fuels the work I do today.

And I realize that I'm so much better at helping grieving people - rather than the sick and dying. I can truly help with spiritual and emotional pain. But I can't relieve physical pain and I can't bear to see that kind of intense physical suffering - especially in young people who only months ago were vibrant and full of life.

I guess I'm still traumatized from taking care of my young husband Paul in my 20s as he died from colon cancer. It's clear that I have some kind of post-traumatic stress syndrome: it makes me want to run from the sight of physical suffering.

Last night I kept feeling like I might throw up when I first walked into her room and saw tubes everywhere, the oxygen tank, and the pain on her face as she struggled to sit up a little in her bed to greet me.

I had to work so hard to focus on her spirit, her beautiful radiant undamaged soul, and not on her body. A big part of me just wanted to run out crying into the night, to stand under the stars, to look at beauty instead of pain.

But instead I took a deep breath, opened my heart and sat down beside her - with love as my intention. Our heart to heart conversation helped calm her - and I hope our future conversations will help her release fear and find an inner peace about crossing over.

I shared many stories with her of the departed coming back to show me that life continues and that death is not the end of anything.

I'm so deeply grateful to those spirits - Paul, Crissie, my dad and so many many others who've made it so abundantly clear that we are all souls who come here for a brief physical experience to evolve consciousness - and that crossing over - taking the final breath - is simply an act of love - of returning to the divine realms from which we came.

I'm so grateful for every moment of this lifetime that has pushed me to recognize this truth and for all the sacred teachers I've had along the way.

And last night, my dying friend loved listening to those stories of departed spirits showing up, and she wanted to hear them again and again. She cried and cried as she listened - as her heart broke wide open.

To all the nurses, hospice workers, healers and physicians who care for the dying - I honor you so much for what you do in the world. It's the hardest and best job there is. Nothing else compares.

I'm so inadequate in the face of other's physical suffering. I have to fight the impulse to run and instead focus on their spirit - which is after all what my work is here.

Writing this has helped me process - not the visit itself - but my visceral reaction to seeing my dying friend. Writing has always helped me heal pain and step into wisdom - to see things more clearly. It's why I write. And maybe now I can resist the pull of Eileen Fisher, of seeking superficial comfort in the face of pain, of longing for beauty instead of what is...

12

Using Grief to Heal Others

There are many souls here who are struggling with the pain of losing a loved one. The experience of heart-wrenching grief is greater now than ever before because consciousness is more evolved and human life is more valued. Love has become more altruistic and prevalent, so death is more painful to those left behind.

This is all part of consciousness shifting. Grief is the great teacher that demands we search our souls for a wiser perspective or lose our way in gut-wrenching pain. Even when we turn to drugs and alcohol for comfort, we eventually find the path of awakening. The disabling physical imbalances caused by toxic substances demand healing. Everything brings us to healing, sooner or later. You can choose your pathway. But the destination is the same for everyone.

Many souls agree to leave early in order to awaken their large soul posses (the loved ones they leave behind). These enlightened souls come to earth in human form for a brief moment of recognition, a short life time with their loved ones. They arrive with a pre-planned early exit. Once they cross over, they work hard from the other side to enlighten and heal their loved ones left behind.

If you've been blessed with soul growth precipitated by the early loss of a loved one, reach out for guidance from your departed. Trust that they're around you offering love and support when you need it. Keep moving forward on your soul journey learning what you came here to learn so that you may join them in higher consciousness.

Consciousness is shifting. There are countless people in powerful places currently aligning with divinity and making decisions that impact everyone's growth. These evolved souls on earth inspire a sacred perspective – they encourage the divine view. You are part of this awakening. You're being asked to pick up your divine lens. If at first pain and grief overwhelms you and you struggle to find greater meaning, ultimately you'll learn that you can reach for the truth and activate your divine lens. Whenever you do this, your life gets better, your pain diminishes, and you begin to help everyone around you awaken.

As this divine perspective spreads amongst us, awakening each one, it ultimately will relieve all suffering on earth. When we shift into higher consciousness our enlightenment transforms darkness. We're reaching a tipping point of awakening right now on Planet Earth.

Alone with your grief, however, you may wonder if you'll be able to make it on your own after your beloved has died. It's completely natural to wonder this. You're in the midst of your greatest soul challenge; the lesson you planned for your earth adventure has arrived at your doorstep. Yet within this tragic moment, within your darkest despair - lives the purpose of your journey.

Your beloved watches over you every day and walks beside you. Yet your ego lens perspective, tells you the opposite. The ego tells you that you're all alone, abandoned, grief stricken and will never be truly happy again. Your divine self tells you a different story, but grief drowns out your inner whisper.

Going through the motions of your old life with the same job, friends, and hobbies will now leave you feeling empty - even though that life once filled you with contentment.

You're meant to change everything now, to shake it all up and grow. This devastating loss was designed by your higher self to break your old life apart, rip it down the seams, and make you start anew. This is for your highest good, even if you can't see that today.

Someday when you've had enough despair, your brave new direction will reveal itself. Taking this path less traveled will bring you love, joy and meaningful work. It will bring you closer to who you came here to be. You'll be guided into the dawn that you've been longing for. But it's up to you to say yes.

Deep inside, layered beneath your grief, lives your innate joy – also known as the soul. When your depression lifts, you can feel joy pulsing within. Your soul is delighted that this pivotal event has finally arrived and that you're in it now - in the thick of the lesson. Saying yes to this moment will open your heart greater than anything you've experienced before.

Your beloved's agreement was to exit before you so that you could find your power, break away from conventional thinking, and do your greatest work. You'll find salvation through helping others.

You've long known that you have healing gifts inside of you. There's miraculous love in the casual conversations you share with others who are hurting. Boldly offering your gift of wisdom to the world is your next step.

Once you intend for this inner gift to become your purpose and to provide income, it will open to you. You'll offer your healing presence fearlessly and be recognized for your meaningful work.

You'll quit the job that no longer serves you and find your way to your most meaningful career. This miracle will happen because it's meant to be, and your life will fill with grace. Your soul desires this alignment.

On your morning walk when you crest a hill and see the shimmer of new sun on the lake, you can feel this joyful possibility within. You take a sip of it with your morning coffee. It waits for you to say yes.

Just one step forward is all it takes, one prayer for guidance, one asking breath and one moment of courage. Your departed beloved applauds you. When you step towards his soul at the end, all pain is healed. You'll feel proud of the way you walked up the final hill and stepped into the light that changed everything.

It seemed so hard at the time, you'll remember. I know, I know, he'll say holding you with love greater than you've ever known. He will be God, and your beloved, and your divinity all in one moment of recognition.

ON THE DAY my father died, he appeared vividly while I meditated. I didn't yet know he had died. But when he appeared during my meditation, I picked up the phone and called the hospital where my brother confirmed that he had just had a heart attack.

While the doctors and nurses performed desperate CPR procedures, and my family members cried and held on to each other, dad was already free of his body – appearing to me young and playful as he had been 40 years earlier. He made me laugh out loud in my meditation before I realized that the apparition in front of me was his soul and that he had just crossed over.

If you're grieving a loved one, quiet your mind and be still. It's only in the silence that your loved one can comfort you - when you're receptive and open-hearted.

Why can't we see our loved ones all the time? Primarily because our left-brains, our cynical ego minds, distract us with worry, doubt and fear. We need our left-brain logic minds for these earthly lifetimes. They filter out the distractions of the divine realms so we can function in the physical world and accomplish what we came to do here.

Our shared goal is to merge this dense physical realm with the highest realms of love and light. When this merger is fulfilled, we'll all reap the sensual beauty of life on earth while still consciously connected to our divinity. You agreed to be part of this consciousness shift. The pain you feel today is your gift of opportunity to shift perspectives.

To connect to the departed, first quiet your logical left-brain. Meditation is the most effective way to consistently accomplish this.

In my career I work with grieving clients nearly everyday. When I'm aligned with higher self, I feel heart opened and connected to a reality greater than our physical world. It's a dimensional shift that occurs when I listen to a grieving person tell their story of loss.

As their words and tears flow, I'm pulled into another dimension where I can sense and sometimes see their departed loved ones. This process is like surrendering to a river of awareness that originates far beyond my mind. I hear words from their loved ones and their guides telling me what to say. It feels like a warm embrace.

When I'm later asked why I said certain things, I have no idea. I can't explain the process. It's not a logical left-brain experience. It's a dialogue with the divine. I feel marinated in love during the experience.

You're absolutely capable of channeling this healing wisdom for yourself from your departed and from your guides. It's a simple shift into your divine lens perspective. The ego must be surrendered to hear the truth. I often use writing as a tool for accessing this higher consciousness.

Begin the process with a sincere request for loving guidance and a clearing of the mind through meditation. Then pick up your pen and begin writing quickly, without editing. As your ego steps out of the way, your higher self takes the pen and writes words that flow from beyond the conscious mind. These words of wisdom will help you heal and re-open your connection to the divine.

Trust this inner voice that comforts when all else is stripped away, when your tears have left you quiet and empty. When you find yourself alone, broke, divorced, fired, and bereft, you may finally be willing to listen to the voice of your soul.

This inner voice is your flawless navigator, your compass in the storm. It's your ticket to happiness and your reason for being. Whenever you write from this inner voice, or speak fearlessly from your heart, unconcerned about judgment, you untether your wisdom.

Your soul is the bird. Your ego is the cage. Your soul is a fearless, wild and beautiful bird. Your ego is a tiny cage. Open the door of your mind and set it free.

From My Soul to Yours: Don't become a hungry ghost

Her face was paper thin and stretched into deep lines of grief that widened as she spoke – telling her story of a son, an avid hiker, a lover of mountains, coming home one day with an unusual bruise and dying in her arms a year later from Leukemia.

She was strong – a nurse who worked all day in a hospital and cared for her son at home. I'll find the best doctor, the best treatment, she would say – escorting him on rounds to places where physicians pondered the next great idea and nurses held her and cried.

Now she sits before me in a room of grieving others. "I don't want to benefit in any way from his death," she says through choking tears. "I don't want to be happy…"

But beside her rises a light beam, a joyful son shaking his head at her pain, wrapping his arms around her. No, he whispers. That's not it. Not the lesson….

He sends his thoughts through me now with a rush of words. I feel his fearless soul, unconventional, never wanting to live within the rules, not meant for a long stay, only a brief visit to tie up some loose ends and help his loved ones wake up to a deeper meaning, a bigger picture that they were missing in their focus on survival.

He hiked when he should have been studying. He skied when he should have worked. He knew what was essential. He broke all the rules while his parents carried on in their disappointments - working hard to pay the bills and not much more.

"Don't become a hungry ghost," he wrote to her on his last day.

"I don't know what that means," his mother cries. Her heart is fierce and her love for him is a wave of pain that crashes across the room – knocking the others over in tears.

When she's told and told her story and is ready to sit in silent meditation, to receive, she begins writing. And finally writing furiously. And smiling.

When the group share their writings, they share the profound words of their loved ones on the other side – urging the ones left behind to live with love and embrace the divine picture of spirits on a brief visit here… some briefer than others.

I did hear from him, she says softly. The hungry ghost is the lost soul, forgetting that they're divine and here on purpose to grow she says reading from her page of notes.

The others in the room nod and share the wisdom they received from their loved ones on the other side. None of the messages tell them to be sad, to give up, to be angry... even though that's how the ones left behind have felt.

They pass their writings around and marvel at how the words from beyond are healing and empowering – for everyone. No matter the mess of death. No matter the suffering. The energy is playful and joyous in these writings passed from griever to griever.

They each tell their stories of loss again on the last day. This time their faces are plump and radiant, clear, smiling, laughing at things they've heard from their departed. The heavy sadness has left the room – flying out the door like a wind swept fog.

I know he's with me and he's watching me and I've got to get my life in gear, says the mom. I'm going to quit my hospital job, be a nursing consultant and work part time at hospice, she says. This way I can help people from what I've learned. It would make me happy to do that work.

Her face is shiny and young like a child holding a birthday gift, excited to open it and happy to be alive. It's her beginning. Her rebirth.

What a lifetime you've had, brave soul!

Many wonderful things have happened to you but you've also experienced many painful events. You've tried to live right, learn and evolve, bring love and gratitude to your relationships. You've embraced yourself as a spiritual explorer and sought answers in alignment with your higher self.

You've also known great loss, utter heartbreak and huge disappointment. Things beyond your control have happened that set you back - especially when you were young and struggling to find your way in the midst of fear and doubt.

When your beloved died, you fell off the edges of the world from grief and despair. But you slowly found your way back into the light.

Congratulations! You're evolving exactly as you came here to do. You're experiencing the lessons you agreed to experience in order to grow and heal. You made soul agreements with your departed loved ones before this lifetime began - knowing that their departure would break your heart wide open. That's exactly what you needed to experience for your highest good. Your beloveds were also fulfilling their highest good through their early departure. This is the gift of your pain though you may not see it today.

What you hold in your heart is the pearl of enlightenment that you came to awaken in this lifetime. All of us came here holding this pearl of wisdom, carrying it in our hearts, its essence vibrating within us to raise our consciousness even while we walk here amongst the dense energy, the heavy curtain of forgetfulness that exists on this realm.

This pearl lives within each of us - waiting to be activated, awakened, so we can fulfill our mission here and evolve – helping others along the way.

You may find yourself sleeping as your days fill with routine, as you follow rules handed to you by others, as you feel un-empowered and like a victim on your journey. At those moments you are not awake. You are sleep walking. Forgetting who you are and why you came here; a forgetful ghost going through the motions of physical existence.

Love will activate your pearl. Not the act of receiving love – although that helps - the act of giving love. Opening your heart in moments of great fear and offering love to those people and situations you fear most. Now your pearl is fully activated and pulsing in divine order. You're in alignment. You're vibrating at such a high frequency that now you're an alchemist, changing the forms of people and things around you. Changing your form from dense and heavy - to light-filled and translucent. You have activated your divine lens.

This is the secret to all healing.

You're capable of living fully this way here on earth, though few accomplish it. Jesus, Buddha, St Francis of Assisi, Gandhi and others are examples of beings who accomplished this and by doing so brought our collective consciousness to a new level.

Pain, deep heart ripping pain, is your other option for activating your pearl, awakening fully here and shifting everything and everyone in your life. This occurs during grief, the death of a child, a sibling, a spouse or career devastation, bankruptcy, and losing everything you care about.

Great soul growth inevitably occurs when the person you've built your life around betrays you and leaves you lost and broken. It also occurs when you betray your highest self with violence, manipulation, abuse, and lies that ultimately leave you on your knees in a terrifying moment of realization of who you've become. When everything is stripped away we find our souls again.

You might believe that you're a victim to tragic losses. Or you might believe that life itself is tragic and random, that bad things happen to good people. You might believe that your pain has been caused by others and now you're drowning in blame and anger.

Here's the truth: You brought with you a soul plan for these difficult lifetime lessons. Agreements were made before this lifetime began for everyone's highest good. You agreed to all of this. You knew the pain would rip you apart and give you an opportunity to wake up and re-align with higher self.

You also knew that without these painful events, you wouldn't evolve as you intended. You realized that these tragedies would break you free of old patterns that you've tried to break for lifetimes. This pain is a gift for you from your highest self.

Put on your divine lens and ask, how can I see this pain differently? What is the lesson in my pain? How can I use this pain as an opportunity to gain wisdom and connect with my soul, to love better, and help others from what I've learned?

Once you're thinking this way, you've activated your divine lens. Answers will flow from your highest self. New choices will arrive that beckon you to move in a positive direction. Fresh opportunities will allow you to live better, love better, and do work that enlightens and heals others. You'll understand how to live in alignment with your soul's wisdom. It's the only way you'll want to live.

This is, after all, what you came here to learn. Hiding from your pain with drugs, alcohol, food or sex doesn't help you become who you came here to be. These fruitless acts only muddle your journey, pull you down into the dense energy and make it harder for you to connect to divinity.

Ask yourself: **what if my greatest and most meaningful work is to offer to others what I wish had been offered to me in my moment of greatest pain?**

Ask yourself: **What if the purpose of my grief is to confront the toughest questions: Who am I? Why am I here? Where has my departed gone? Questions that push me to finally align with my divinity.**

Asking those questions sets you on the path of growth and spiritual exploration that will change your life and carry you into the light. Asking those questions is the beginning of your true work and your soul's journey.

Ask these questions today and don't stop asking until you find answers that resonate deep within as sacred and true. Then you'll have found a deep and powerful connection to soul, to your divinity. Your heart will begin vibrating with fearless love for everyone including yourself - as a divine being on a sacred journey of evolution.

Now, you've arrived at the place you've been looking for most of your life.

Let me tell you a story...

Recently after traveling to San Francisco to teach my Bridges to Heaven: Talking to Loved Ones on the Other Side grief shifting workshop I discovered that when United put me on a different flight to San Francisco because of weather that it cancelled my entire ticket and I had no flight reservation home to Colorado. My ego immediately got upset because no one at United had mentioned anything about cancelling my entire ticket when they re-routed me to a new flight.

I called United and spent 45 minutes on the phone with an extraordinarily sweet agent, who in spite of my initial grumpiness, was patient and kind and fixed everything. He got me back on the same flight with no extra fees.

He told me at the end of the call that he put extra energy into helping me because his departed mother whispered to him to help me out. He had no idea what I do for a living or that I'd just spent

85

two days teaching a Talking to Loved Ones on the Other Side - grief workshop.

I suddenly understood the divine order that had been in action to put us together on the phone. We spent another ten minutes connecting with his mom and discussing his future great work. He was crying with happiness at the end of the call.

The amazing thing is that almost everyone in the workshop I had taught that day was grieving their mom. (Each group I work with usually has a distinct theme that becomes apparent as we hear everyone's story of loss. We had laughingly called our group that weekend the dead moms club. I kept telling my students that the room was filled with loving mother energy. You could feel it in the air.)

Through the grace of Divine Order, I got to end my day with this amazing conversation with another soul who was grieving his mom. I feel so blessed to do what I do in the world. And Divine Order blows me away. Always.

More Divine Order travel stories...

I recently taught a grief-shifting workshop at Kripalu Retreat Center in Massachusetts. When I went to board my flight home to Colorado from the Albany airport I discovered my flight had been cancelled due to engine problems and there were no more flights out that evening.

After waiting in line for too long to get the airline to book me into a local hotel for the night, I found my own room in a nearby hotel where I had a lovely relaxing evening before flying home the next morning. Back home in Colorado, I emailed United requesting financial compensation for my hotel room.

The next day, United airlines called me and the agent said she'd read my email to customer service requesting compensation for paying for my own hotel room when my flight was cancelled.

She said she'd read the signature on my email and learned that I was the author of Bridges to Heaven: True Stories of Loved Ones on the Other side and had looked up my work on the web. She was grieving the recent loss of her dad.

We had a healing conversation about her departed dad and her mom who talks to spirit. Thanks to her, United is sending me an electronic coupon for another ticket that's double the amount I expected. And I got to help ease the grief of another soul.

I'm convinced that the spirits of our departed bring us into the presence of those who can help us – as long as we keep an open heart and take the opportunity for healing that divine order presents. I'm happy to have my travel rearranged by spirits of the departed so that I can connect to those who need healing.

13

GLORIOUS HEALTH AND WELL-BEING

When the ego-mind rules, illness occurs. This is the soul's way of getting your attention and turning your focus inward. Your body may manifest heart palpitations, high blood pressure, cancer, viruses and chronic conditions as a nudge from your higher self to wake up and re-align.

Accessing your divine lens aligns you with the wisdom of your soul and empowers your immune system to flawlessly perform its job of keeping you healthy. When this alignment occurs, chronic illness heals, inflammation reverses and viruses mend.

This connection between body, mind and spirit is well documented in scientific literature. You've also experienced this connection in your day-to-day life. Whenever you're behind the wheel of a car getting angry or frustrated with other drivers, your heart rate and blood pressure skyrocket. You may notice your heart pounding, your palms getting sweaty and your breathing becoming shallow. This is proof of how your inner perspective impacts your physical body. In this moment of frustration, your immune system is diminished and all bodily systems are thrown out of whack. You feel stressed and exhausted at the same time.

Pretend for a moment that instead of sitting in traffic, you're walking on the warm sand of your favorite beach, listening to the sound of gentle rolling waves, feeling the soft breeze of a summer day against your skin. You have no worries. All your problems have been solved. Take a deep breath and truly feel the relief of that moment. Notice your heart rate slowing, your breath regulating, and your sense of inner peace returning. You've shifted into your divine lens.

Which lens do you use most often? And how is it serving you and your health? Which perspective feels better? Your divine lens elevates the immune system and reduces stress. Your ego lens sets off an inflammation response that triggers everything from heart disease to cancer. You get to choose your perspective -whether you're sitting in traffic or facing the loss of a loved one.

Your health challenges are rich with soul lessons and perfectly designed to help you evolve in just the way you need to. Inside each unique health challenge lives the perfect solution if you're willing to choose the solution and embrace your divine lens perspective. When you refuse the lesson, your soul activates a more powerful wake-up call to get your attention. Within a lifetime, you're given many challenging opportunities to re-align with your soul's wisdom.

But if you continually fail to align with higher self, your body will provide even greater nudges to get your attention until the soul has awakened. After a terrifying health diagnosis, you'll suddenly ask the good questions and look for new answers so the crisis can be used for your highest good. Your body has provided you with a major perspective shift and a moment of heart opening possibility.

Will you act on it? If you don't, another lesson will be graciously offered for your highest good, simply to help you awaken. You are not your body; it's only the shell holding your soul. Surrendering to the lessons of the body can bring you deeply in alignment with soul, even in your final breath. Your last moment on earth can be your great awakening. Nothing is over until the soul leaves the body. Each lifetime is a journey of endless reinvention and growth.

Your body is a vehicle for your most powerful lessons because it can't be ignored. You can try to ignore your soul, but the body has a disruptive voice. You'll hear it loud and clear in spite of your refusal to grow. It will wake you from a deep sleep and drench you in sweat until you surrender to a new point of view.

Once your body is injured or ill, you'll take action to change your life. You'd probably also change your life to save the physical health of someone you love. But it's disturbing how little we'll risk to save our emotional and spiritual selves.

The body can't be ignored whether it's splayed across a highway, butchered in a gunfight, or ravaged with cancer. When we see a physical wound in ourselves or others, we take positive action. The same should be true of our spiritual and emotional wounds.

As physical bodies in a physical world, we often ignore what we can't see. Yet when we look beyond the surface to see another's true essence, to see beyond the physical self, we're acting in alignment with our divinity. We're connecting soul to soul. And what we find in those moments is our own divinity reflected back to us. We remember that we're souls on a shared journey, wearing different costumes and playing different roles, all of us wounded and gifted. But our essence is the same.

The act of reaching out to save another saves you. Our bodies are hardwired to feel good when we help others – no matter whether we're saving them physically, spiritually or emotionally. An act of kindness boosts the immune system. How perfectly we're designed to recognize the divine essence of others – and to align with our own sacredness.

Many conventional medical doctors address the soul of healing. But many physicians only think of the body as a machine to be fixed, a chemistry to be balanced. Spiritual and alternative healers address both body and soul. They seek to understand the intricate interplay between our physical, spiritual and emotional health. Any physician who looks at the body as more than a physical system, is a true healer.

Your soul is always in charge. To heal your body, you must also do the inner work of realigning with highest self. Seek to understand how and why you've disconnected from your wisdom. Examine your past to see choice points where you could have taken a different path. Make adjustments in your beliefs and take steps in a new direction. This is essential for healing.

Your soul is calling you to shift into your divine lens. Your previous point of view has made you sick. You're being nudged to quit the job that's toxic, start the business you've dreamed of, return to school or walk away from a toxic relationship. Your illness won't prevent you from taking these steps. On the contrary, making these changes will save your life.

Changing your lifestyle inside and out creates a powerful paradigm shift that makes true healing possible. The energy of the food you eat affects both your physical and emotional health. Processed food, even if it carries an impressive nutrition label, has no life force. Its life-giving properties have been removed long ago. Fresh, untreated, unprocessed foods, like vegetables from your local farmers market, carry a high vibrational frequency - which accelerates healing. Empty processed foods deplete the immune system because the body expends tremendous energy trying to digest them.

We each have several pre-determined possible choice points for exiting a lifetime. At each choice point, the soul is reminded of what it came here to accomplish. We're asked if we'll be able to succeed in our mission or if we've completed the journey. We can choose to stay, or to hit the reset button, start another lifetime, and return to the highest realms for healing.

If you have a serious illness, this may be your pre-determined exit point. Your soul may be deciding if you can accomplish what you came here to do and fulfill your soul's mission.

The world tells us that death is random. It's not. It's the soul's choice. We exit for reasons that can't always be understood by others. If we've been living off-path, lost in fear, or drowning in self-indulgence, our soul may choose to leave and re-group in the higher realms. If we've lived mostly in alignment with highest self, we may have accomplished our mission and choose to exit early – knowing that our early exit will launch our loved ones into tremendous soul growth - born from pain.

This is why a child's soul may choose to die young. The child is highly evolved and they've accomplished what they came here for. Their early exit provides their grieving loved ones an opportunity to search for sacred meaning and to experience accelerated soul growth before returning to the divine to reunite with their child.

When someone lives well into old age, it often means they were determined to keep learning even as their physical being disintegrated. This can either be a sign of a highly evolved soul or a stubborn ego who needed to experience physical deterioration in order to shift perspective. In the final days, this soul may experience tremendous spiritual awakening as they depart the physical body – even when it doesn't appear so from the outside. They may appear shut down and unaware. But the soul is always processing. Things are seldom as they appear.

Your loved one may have been suffering from dementia, but their soul was hard at work, often ascending into the higher realms for guidance and returning to the body for moments of awakening. This inner growth can occur in the midst of dementia, coma or brain damage. Consciousness does not live in the mind; only in the soul.

During coma, the soul leaves the body to regroup in the divine where a decision is made as to whether the soul mission has been or will be fulfilled. The decision is made for everyone's highest good.

If a person dies from a long illness like cancer, their soul has chosen to use physical suffering to purify a part of themselves that they wanted to bring into the light for healing. The illness allows them to loosen their attachment to the physical and align fully with their divinity. When they cross over, the physical suffering will have served its purpose to open the heart and cleanse away negativity.

We don't need to choose suffering. But it's a choice our soul can make for our highest good. This choice, made before the lifetime begins, is created in cooperation with the loved ones caring for the dying person. The caretakers agree to become part of this experience for their own evolution. Those who witness suffering without being able to ease it, experience deep despair - which teaches divine compassion. The soul benefits whichever role we play; to suffer or to ease the suffering of others.

14

SUCCESS AND MEANINGFUL WORK

You still have something important to do – even if you can't see it right now. Even when you feel lost and pointless, without direction, floating in grief – that great thing still lives inside of you. Deep down.

When the time is right and the world is ready and you've learned what you needed to learn – your great gift will come pouring out of you like an Arkansas Spring flood, like a hurricane downpour, unstoppable and urgent.

It will save every heart, crack the world wide apart, pour light into darkness, open minds, heal souls and change lives – especially yours.

It's the gift you agreed to bring into this lifetime. Nobody else brought it. Only you. You signed up for this one – orchestrated the precise childhood to bring this gift to birth inside of you, designed the perfect pain to wake you up and break your heart wide open and turn everything you've learned into soaring wisdom that sings in just this key, this chord, that nobody else can strike, that nobody else could possibly deliver, that nobody else is capable of sharing in your exact way.

This gift has your number on it – no one else's. It fits perfectly into the puzzle slot that's waiting empty now. Not until every empty slot of this puzzle is filled can we change this world, light it up with consciousness and shift it over into bliss.

When everyone brings their unique piece to the table we all win. And right now everyone is wondering exactly where your piece is and when you'll bring it to the puzzle because your gift is the tipping point, the one we've all been waiting for, and it changes everything.

So you've been laid off...

Maybe you've been laid off or fired or you didn't get that new job. You feel like the wind has been knocked out of you; it's a punch to the gut. The job and career you've steadily built for years has now been unfairly taken away.

When you first hear the news, you'll notice a brief moment of calm because your ego mind is momentarily stunned into silence. This gap allows you to hear your powerful intuition and higher-self whispering: "Everything is okay. Something better is waiting. This is all in divine order for your highest good."

Your soul's wisdom speaks up the moment your ego mind receives a swift blow and is temporarily stunned into silence. We sometimes call this being in "a state of shock." We feel numb and the mind is quiet.

But very soon, within minutes, the ego mind fires up and whispers: "I don't deserve this! I'll never find another good job. How dare they! I'll lose my home!"

Your ego mind is launching its battle of survival exactly as it was designed to. This is the mind you agreed to have when you took a physical body for this incarnation. Yet it's only half of your mind.

The other half of your mind holds the doorway to your highest self, your divine intuition and your true essence. In brief gaps when the ego is silenced, you can hear your higher-self whispering the truth.

Grab hold of that deep inner voice. It's the wisdom of your soul. Listen to it before the ego mind overpowers it with fear. Shortly after you get bad news of any kind, the ego mind shifts into full-blown desperation. That brief silent gap before ego steps in is your golden opportunity for salvation.

Unrestrained, the ego mind can push you to the edge of sanity. During crisis, your sanity will depend on how well you've learned to quiet the mind through meditation or other forms of spiritual practice.

When you indulge the fear, you allow it to grow stronger until it becomes your boss. If you haven't developed the mental discipline of quieting fear thoughts, ego will reign supreme over your higher self. It will provoke you to defend yourself at all costs and trust no one. This ego-based attitude will destroy your happiness, future success and relationships - until you recognize that fear is your only enemy.

Everything changes the moment you listen to your soul's wisdom; it's a simple request: "Please show me my soul's lesson in this crisis and help me move through it with love and courage."

That simple request calls wisdom to your side, fills you with light, opens your heart, quiets your mind, and reveals an enlightening new perspective on the situation. You'll feel empowered from within. Your inner victim will settle down.

Your soul created this moment to allow you to step up to your wisdom, awaken into love, and embrace spirituality. You're not being punished. You're not a victim. You've done nothing wrong. It's simply a reinvention point designed for your highest good. By embracing the lesson of the job loss, you'll discover a new career that brings you to a greater level of meaningful work and abundance.

You're not a victim to the economy, your manager, or corrupt politicians. You're a divine being who created this moment to shake up old patterns and free yourself to become who you came here to be. You've been stuck for too long and this is your wake-up call.

You didn't come here to live in fear, to be hidden or unimportant. You came to be grand and fearless, bold and awake, and infused with wisdom. When you activate your divine lens, this is who you are.

Your ego, nurtured by teachers, priests, ministers and well-meaning loved ones, is your "should-do" self. It says: This is who you "should be" in order to please others. This is what I "should do" to be practical and survive.

Your divine self whispers: This is what I know to be true about my gifts and who I came here to be. It will take courage to follow this path, but it feels right.

Your ego and divine self are often in direct opposition, pulling you in conflicting directions. Your should-be, should-do voice is the truth-slayer; it's a defeater of wisdom and confidence. You can hush it with a prayer in the night or a heart felt request for divine intervention.

Everything shifts as soon as you say: "I will not live in fear. When fear arises, I'll reach for love instead. I'll find courage within my heart."

This aligns you with your divine self rather than the ego. Higher consciousness lives within you, always. It's part of your DNA. You've grown used to ignoring this higher consciousness because the ego mind deletes it immediately with fear thoughts. You've allowed this pattern to continue for too long. It takes courage to break it.

What is courage to a person who trudges along untethered from their soul's longing? What is love to someone who finds pleasure only in the mundane? Those who fear the richness of fearless love and courageous choices are asleep. Their souls walk through this world unaware.

Courage is essential to living your best life. It serves you well to make irrational career choices as you pursue what you know to be true about yourself. This world will scare you away from boldness. It will diminish your dreams with fear. You may reset your course to be practical above all else - believing that this will save you. The opposite is true. Your compromised choices will lead nowhere. They'll feel safe enough to grab hold of. Yet fear never leads to success. A leap of faith is always required.

Eventually you'll end up separated from true self. By honoring the ego above all else, you'll lose your connection to the divine. Without this inner compass, you'll find yourself adrift on ravaged seas, alone and hopeless. Your separation from divinity will damage relationships, destroy careers, make you sick, and empty your bank account. When everything is taken away, when you're disgusted with this mundane world, you might finally make a different choice.

At any moment, you can choose to live in alignment with higher self - rather than ego. This changes everything. As soon as you surrender ego, you find the fulfillment, happiness and success you've always sought.

Each lifetime contains a series of awakenings. If we embrace the lessons within each challenge, we find our way. We stay on path. We're given many opportunities to change direction, reinvent and rethink - each time we hit a crisis.

The journey of awakening is harder if we resist it until we're in our 50s and 60s. Surrendering ego becomes harder as we age because we've become addicted to our fear-based point of view. Our courage to choose the unknown determines our future. The sooner we choose the more enlightened perspective of the soul, the sooner we find happiness.

Encourage your children to search for answers that inspire them rather than diminish their self-esteem. Teach them to use the divine lens perspective whenever they face a choice. Model these wise choices for your children. They learn by watching you, not by listening to your words. If they see you living in fear, they absorb your negative pattern - no matter what you teach them. If they've been raised with authentic love, they'll find their way to courage.

Our children push us to the next level of our soul growth - not the other way around. When we see fear reflected in our children's choices, we realize our own shortcomings. We're meant to learn from this and redirect our lives.

Children illuminate the flaws in our journeys; the places where we haven't listened to soul, and the moments we've given ourselves away to ego. Their actions say to us: "Your refusal to grow is reflected in my own pain and failures. Heal me by healing yourself. Live in alignment with your divinity, so I can do the same."

Which lens did you choose this morning?

Pick your viewpoint carefully. Because the one you choose today determines everything. It pushes you down a path that becomes your story. What will your story be at the end? Will it be a tale of meaningless work and choices made from fear? Or will it be a grand and bold tale of courage, wisdom and laughter on the path less traveled? You get to choose....

Remember, it takes baby steps to climb any mountain. You may see what you came here to do and the greatness of it may overwhelm you. You need to focus on what's right in front of you today and ask, **"What is one small step I can take today that will begin to turn my life in this new direction?"**

If you ask that question everyday and keep moving forward with little steps, you *will always* arrive where you're meant to be – doing your great work.

If today you feel joyful about your career and are creating abundance – you're on path. However in a few years, changes may be required. We all have many reinvention points in our lives that are designed to nudge us forward and help us kick it up to the next level.

Growth and change ARE required here. They're part of our shared human experience. If you embrace these changes, trust your intuition rather than your monkey mind, and gracefully step up to the next level, your life just gets better and better.

Our broken hearts and disappointments are meant to wake us up to our great potential and help us reinvent and go in a new direction - the right direction. The more off-path we are, the greater the nudges will be.

If you're a very old soul who came in to do great work and help raise consciousness (and you ARE), you'll get big wake up calls (job loss, divorce, bankruptcy, illness) until you stop hiding and start living true to your highest self. When you're ready to listen, your intuition will guide you flawlessly in the right direction.

We should all be thanking the bosses who fire us and the lovers who break our hearts. These are our greatest teachers. They agreed before this lifetime began to help us remember who we are. The pain they cause in our lives forces us to ask the good questions: Who am I? Why am I here? Where do I go when I die? Did I come here to do great work? How can I navigate differently now to find my true purpose?

Until we ask these questions, we can't find our way. Sometimes it takes great pain to wake us up to our purpose here – though it doesn't have to. But pain seems to be what gets our attention easily.

15

RELATIONSHIPS ILLUMINATED

Have you ever "recognized" someone the moment you first met? You're recognizing a soul mate – someone you've been through many lifetimes with and have made a soul agreement with. This person is part of your soul posse.

The agreement, made before your lifetime began, went something like this: I'll recognize you, embrace your true essence, and push you to evolve (through love and pain). We'll become spiritual partners exploring new ideas. We'll push each other to grow.

When your soul recognizes another, you feel the spark of this agreement you've made. It awakens you. Yet the ego often misinterprets this spark as what the world calls romantic love – a happily ever-after fairy tale.

Both romantic love and great friendship begin with the first flush of soul recognition. You believe you've found someone who understands and supports you completely. You have. But a soul mate embraces your soul's essence – not your ego. This relationship (whether it's a great friendship or a deeply passionate love) only thrives when the soul is honored, when the conversations are meaningful, and when you process the world together through your divine lens.

When you're with a soul mate, you'll experience many reinventions together in a lifetime. Through them all, he or she will encourage you to grow and to align with your highest wisdom. You will do the same for your partner. If either of you stop supporting each other's inner growth, the relationship ends. The agreement is broken.

If you prioritize money, jobs, and material possessions instead of the soul-to-soul connection, your love diminishes. You begin to feel trapped, shut-down and afraid. When your soul's growth is no longer being served, you'll both find a way to fulfill your growth elsewhere.

If anger, blame, fear and criticism become the primary energies flowing between you in any relationship, you'll find a way out – for your highest good and the good of your partner. You may choose to have an affair, treat your spouse poorly, or shut down and become deeply depressed. Or you may become abusive and hypercritical. You may also manifest an illness. All of these are acts spurred by your soul's longing to grow and fulfill its mission.

Ego is your greatest enemy in any relationship. Ego focuses only on the flaws of ourselves and others. The ego lens prevents us from seeing the troubled soul behind any misbehavior. And it prevents you from seeing the great potential within yourself.

Choose your partner based on which lens they wear most often: Ego or Divine lens

Years ago, a boyfriend told me he didn't believe in anything beyond the physical and that there was no evidence of a God. I didn't know how to respond. I live with evidence everyday within in my dialogues with the divine and my personal intuitive experiences. This constant conversation inspires me with love and happiness.

I said to him: "Who do you talk to when you're all alone?"

"My mind. It tells me things," he said.

"What kind of things?"

"Sometimes dark and worrisome things and I have anxiety. Other times inspiring ideas, thoughts that make me smile."

"The anxiety thoughts are from your monkey mind," I explained. "But the ones that fill you with happiness and make

100

you smile for no reason – those are from the divine. Try to listen to those more than to the fearful thoughts."

We broke up. He thought I needed fixing. Today I'm happy, fulfilled, married to a man whose spiritual beliefs are in alignment with mine, and my work is meaningful. That ex-boyfriend who thought I needed fixing has fought a lifelong battle with depression and anxiety – both side effects of ego lens living. In the end, it matters which beliefs we embrace and which ones our partners embrace.

Divorce can be an opportunity for realignment with soul's mission. But when negotiations become bogged down with blame and anger, it means both parties are stuck in the ego lens. No one is bringing their soul's wisdom to the conversation and resolution can't occur until this happens.

If you're going through a divorce you can shift the energy to a higher level even if your partner is lost in blame. It's a matter of shifting your intention. During your daily meditation, silently send this intention to your partner:

> **I see your great potential and I'm deeply sorry I was unable to support you in fulfilling it.** *I will not hurt you or diminish your ability to move forward. I recognize that I have a soul connection with you and that my actions towards you come back to me a thousand fold. I won't dwell in anger, blame, fear or depression because that energy does not serve my highest good – or yours.* **I release you fully to your soul's journey – until we meet again and can make each other proud with how we've each evolved. We are now and always will be – soul mates.**

It doesn't matter if your partner reciprocates this intention or not. You're now standing in the light of your soul's integrity – which is the only place you want to be. Because of your courageous energy shift, all good things are now possible. At the end of your lifetime, you'll answer to your highest self for your actions and yours alone. You'll see clearly that there has never been anyone to blame. Your soul made choices every step of the way.

You'll realize that within every moment of your life, including this painful divorce, there was a lesson your soul chose to experience for your highest good. The people who are hurting you the most today are acting in your highest good. They're your soul partners, taking their places exactly as you asked them to, pushing you where you need to go.

When a relationship causes you pain, use this intention:

Thank you worthy opponent for arriving at this moment of my greatest need, when I was finally ready for this profound lesson and ready to break old patterns that have held me back. You must love me very much to help me release these behaviors that my ego has been unable to surrender on its own.

I remember now that I came here to be radiantly loving and wise. My ego was preventing me from being my best self. You've awakened me to remember my highest self and I'm deeply grateful.

Now you're fully capable of healing yourself and helping others heal as you move forward. You're capable of saving a future relationship that has fallen off course, or saving a friend who has lost their way.

When people speak of forgiveness, there is sometimes a sense of one partner feeling superior to the other. But this isn't forgiveness. Forgiveness means saying to someone who hurt you: *I see your soul. I realize we're both on the same journey of evolution doing the best we can. Our agreement is to help each other remember our divinity – through pain and love. I release you to your highest good, with gratitude, until we meet again.*

Here's what you never knew:

The encouraging word you offered to a stranger that rainy day in a coffee shop – saved him. The heartfelt hug you gave to a friend you ran into at the party – healed her. The moment you turned your back on fear and ripped your heart wide open - *changed everything.*

Your one simple act of courage started a ripple of consciousness that spread far beyond you.

At the end you'll see it. All the ripples spreading out, merging and turning into waves of light. You'll see the way your words of wisdom pulled someone to shore – someone you never met – who then reached back and saved your brother, sister, child – who then saved you.

16

FLAWLESS INTUITION: A BYPRODUCT OF THE DIVINE LENS PERSPECTIVE

Once your viewpoint is aligned with soul rather than ego, you suddenly have perfect vision. Nothing is distorted. You see things you've never seen before and didn't know existed – including other dimensions and spirits that you've been ignoring. Your ego lens has been distorting reality for you and has made you doubt that anything beyond the physical world existed.

You've already experienced these other dimensions – even though you may have dismissed them as nonsense. Whenever you opened your heart to another, you gained access to all the inner knowledge and guidance you could ever need. This is called intuition. When you first fell in love you experienced this: You knew when your lover would call. You had dreams of the future that turned out to be true. You had heightened awareness.

Why didn't this awareness last? Because you allowed ego lens to slip back in and distort your perceptions. You allowed your feelings to get hurt, and you became afraid that love wouldn't be returned. You shut your heart in fear.

You fell back into the comfort of ego lens, with its distorted view and fear-based limitations. Now you've grown addicted to this earth-bound perspective - even though it rarely makes you happy.

Intuition is your gut feeling. It is, above all else, a feeling from the heart. It marinates you in confidence, wisdom, and empowerment--never in fear. It's the connection to your true self, your raw, unrefined truth unclouded by the monkey-mind.

It's the shimmer of a spirit in the corner when you turn your head and the dream that wakes you up and stays with you. It's the knowingness that comes when you stop talking. It's the feeling that overpowers you in spite of logic.

It's the voice whispering in your ear, and the nudge you often ignore in deference to being practical. It's your right-brain, expanded consciousness guiding your journey as planned.

But you already know how this will end...

In the brief moments of great joy that you do allow, you know everything you ever need to know. You disappoint your higher self whenever you deny this. Imagine if you embraced your sixth sense as an ally and consulted it everyday for guidance. *"Would I still get everything I need and want?"* asks the ego.

"Yes," says the soul. "You would get everything you came here to experience and everything your soul needs to fulfill its great mission."

"But would I get the car, the house, the bank account, and the love that I long for?" asks the ego.

"Yes, if that's what your soul came to experience for your highest good and to fulfill your magnificent potential," answers the soul. "Your authentic journey is the only path to joy."

"But I long for the things that others who are more successful have," says the ego.

"If those things aren't in alignment with your highest good, they'll never be yours," says the soul. "And you'll overlook the gifts of the journey you've chosen."

Longing for a life that's not yours will push you far from who you came to be and what you came to accomplish. You'll lose your heart and soul in someone else's life. You've already lived many lifetimes with circumstances quite different from this life. You've been rich and you've been poor. You designed each lifetime, including this one, to perfectly empower you to blossom into your greatest self.

You're here to become the greatest version of you and not someone else. This is your true path. It requires feeling more, opening the heart, and thinking less. You're learning to trust your higher self rather than the expectations of those around you. When you succeed, you'll realize the grace of divine order that has always flowed through your life.

You may be afraid of taking the path less traveled. Who will love you then? How will you survive? You ARE different, says your soul. You've never been like anyone else. Trying to hide your unique self and live like others will not get you anywhere good. Love does not exist in false relationships. To hide your gifts is to live the loneliest life you could choose.

Nothing is more painful than hiding your soul from the world.

In the end, you'll be fully revealed as who you came to be and you hope that this revelation won't be on your deathbed when the illusion finally fades and it's too late to change everything.

And you hope it won't be when you're too feeble to do your soul's work. You hope it will be now. Today. Not tomorrow, although tomorrow is never too late.

But today is always better. Today is always the best day; to start everything, change everything, love everyone like you never have before, drop your fear on the ground and forget to pick it up. Because today is juicy and alive and tomorrow may never arrive.

And today is when you planned to finally listen to your soul's wisdom, use your divine lens to see what you never saw, to know everything you've needed to know. Today is the day you meant to transcend all limitation, release all fear, take the big step, throw out the old, embrace your gold, and get it done the way you came here to get it done.

Today is **that** day...

The most powerful way to quiet the monkey mind and access your intuition (your flawless inner guidance) is through 20 minutes of daily meditation. Everyone can find 20 minutes to sit and close their eyes and repeat either a mantra (sacred sound) or a prayer. The purpose is *not* to think, *not* to visualize, and *not* to say affirmations. Instead you're lulling the monkey mind to sleep by giving it the mantra, or sacred words, to repeat.

During meditation, your thoughts will come bursting through the mantra. You can notice them but gently bring your focus back to the mantra. At the end of 20 minutes of redirecting your attention this way, you begin to sink into your "knowingness" - which goes beyond the mental chatter of the fear-based mind. That's the opening of the door to your higher self and your inner guidance – also known as intuition.

Easy Steps to Enhance Your Intuition

1. Shift your view into the divine lens perspective:
Take a breath. Pause. Ask to connect to your higher self.

2. Meditate to quiet the mind:
Close your eyes and repeat sacred mantra or prayer. Keep refocusing the mind away from your thoughts and back to the sacred mantra.

3. Ask for divine guidance:
Say: Please God (or divine guides) help me to quiet my fear mind, open my heart and hear my inner divine guidance. Then listen and write whatever comes to you.

4. Practice intuitive living:
Whenever making a decision picture yourself having made that decision already and living in that future. If it's a small decision like which restaurant to go to, picture yourself there eating your meal. See the room, smell the food. Now notice how that choice makes your body feel. Does it make you smile? Is it energizing? Or does it leave you feeling drained or anxious? Your gut is telling you what the right intuitive choice is: **Practice listening to your gut for little decisions all day long.** Then when you need to make a major life decision, you'll be very good at listening to and trusting your inner guidance system.

17

WHO WILL YOU BECOME?

From My Soul to Yours: What I know to be true

Divine order rules! A doubt-inducing childhood, a sweet husband's early death, countless broken hearts and flawed careers, were all perfectly designed to get me where I came here to go; to help me evolve to my highest state of grace, to know God, and to become who I became. I *mostly* forget this.

When I'm on path and in alignment with divine order, I feel of use to the greater message, the larger truth, the highest good. It moves through me like a ray of light piercing everything, a laser beam opening my heart, filling the pages of my books, conversations with clients, and classrooms where I teach. None of it comes from me – a flawed human like everyone else here. I just finally get out of the way.

When I forget about divine order, nothing makes sense. My sadness is legendary. My hunger is hopeless. Heartbreak brings me to my knees in despair. Everyone betrays me; my mother, brother, sister, lover, friend. I am a boat without a mooring. Fear blocks my inner voice. My mind tricks me. I let it.

When I remember the loving God-ness of our universe, my heart breaks wide open. Sacred wisdom pours through me and showers the world in diamonds - each one forged from the fire of tremendous loss. Forgiveness abounds. I feel held by the angels. Kissed by the Deities.

I adore my mother, brother, sister, lover, friend. I see their painful stories, their enormous grief and astounding gifts. I see how hard they've tried, how endlessly they've worked. I adore them all. The sound of their laughter is the sweetest sound I've ever known. I lift the veil and see into the other realms vividly. I speak out loud to my departed dad, to Paul, Crissie and Marv. It's all good, they whisper. Very good...

When I cross over, I'll apologize for the wasted days here, the endless pain, the soaring doubt and aching exhaustion – the days when I didn't move. My divine beloveds will hold me and tell me that it was all part of the play, the dance of life, and exactly what they expected. They'll remind me that I couldn't have lived here without each moment of deeply felt pain, determined anger, and paralyzing doubt. These profound feelings, they'll explain, led me to my moments of boundless love, soul-shaking awe, inspired wisdom and healing grace.

What I know to be true is this: Our pain is on purpose. Our joy is the gift. Our heart is all that matters. Our mind is a great monkey loose in the forest and running amuck; he must be tamed.

Our truth is inside – always. It's the inner voice that only speaks loud enough when we turn within, tame the savage mind, and surrender assumptions; when we dip a trembling hand into the deepest water that terrifies us most and help someone who is drowning right beside us.

Our truth only speaks up when we see the heartbreak in everyone's journey, the struggle in everyone's life, the pain shared by each family member, the divine inner guidance within each moment. This compassion is the fabric of our universe, it guides us flawlessly through the night. This is all that matters.

Even when we don't know it, when we feel completely alone, there are people who are part of our soul posse who show up in our hour of greatest need and help us in ways we may never know and never see. These soul mate agreements are always working in our favor even when we feel hopelessly abandoned, they're standing where they should be standing and lending a hand in just the way that will save us.

And mostly it's only at the end of our life or in brief glimpses of the divine that we fully see this luminous connection, this brilliant pattern, and know that it's real and that we've always been held in grace. This final knowledge breaks us wide open in speechless, awestruck gratitude - even as we take our last gasping breath and our bodies disintegrate into a million shards of light.

Loving the valleys

When we're at the top, the peak of a cycle, and all is going well, it's tempting to discard our Divine Lens. The ego is winning. We're content to see life as a physical world because we're basking in the glow of worldly success. We're having fun!

As soon as we hit a valley, a great loss, illness or heartbreak, we struggle to find our bearings, until we reach for the Divine Lens. Then we remember the gift of the lesson; we reconnect with our soul's wisdom.

This is the purpose of pain - to remind us of what's important and who we really are. When we love the valley, cherish our Divine Lens view, and embrace the lesson of our pain, we find ourselves happy again and beginning the climb towards another glorious peak.

This is the sweet spot. We're still wearing our Divine Lens, tapped into our inner wisdom, and excited to be moving forward.

If you're in a valley today from job loss or heartbreak, look within, meditate, ask for divine guidance and listen to your soul's wisdom. Take a breath. You can only hear inner guidance when you're quiet, unplugged and receptive.

Become best friends with your inner wisdom and shut out the chatter around you. Once you embrace the view from your higher self, you'll feel peaceful, grateful and openhearted. This is when things will begin shifting in a better direction.

You'll find yourself moving forward with an exciting new summit just ahead. Keep wearing your Divine Lens and cherish the wisdom you've gained in the valley.

Yes it takes effort to reach for your divine lens, to struggle against your cynicism, self doubt and fear. It's much easier to surrender to the negative forces of the world that urge you to indulge in physical experiences and ignore your inner soul whisper. Everyone gives into depression, anger, blame, or disappointment at certain points in their journey.

Why struggle to find wisdom, open-hearted love, or forgiveness? Why rip your heart out and feel the pain you're terrified of feeling? Why search for the deeper meaning of a painful past when it's so much easier to become the angry victim of circumstances?

Here's why: Because each thought you think, each step you take, puts you on a certain path, an intended direction - until you remember who you came here to be.

The further you move down a negative path, the harder it becomes to change directions, live fearlessly and open your heart. The dark and cynical story you tell about life's hardships gets ingrained into your essence. You become burdened with cynicism. You carry the frequency of fear in your voice. Love becomes impossible. Cynicism is then expected of you. It chooses your friends. Changing everything and living courageously becomes a choice you can't imagine making.

Once when you were young, you could imagine taking the path of courage and hope. You could see it as a possibility. You made a brief attempt to take risks, follow your heart and change your life for the better. When you didn't immediately reap success, you decided it wasn't worth the struggle. It was easier to give up, complain, and be afraid. Cynicism is always the easier path.

Like the traveler who sets a safe course, you stayed on the path you'd become most familiar with. For awhile the other path, the one you hadn't chosen, ran parallel to yours. It wouldn't have required a major lifestyle shift to head in that direction. You told yourself that if you changed your mind later, you could still choose that riskier path. But you were having fun where you were. Life was comfortable.

As time went on, you traveled further down the trail you'd chosen, until you found yourself lost in the trees, unable to see the sky. When you looked for the upper trail that once ran parallel, you saw that it had taken a different course, winding steeply up around the mountain towards a peak that rose sharply into the light.

This stirred a memory in you - a memory of once wanting to make that summit, of studying it on a map and dreaming of standing there in that exquisite light - feeling awesome about what you'd accomplished.

But now your trail has taken you deep into the shadows, far beneath the forested sky, and somehow you're more alone than you realized. Joining the other path at this point requires a terrifying change of course. You doubt that you're still strong enough to make such a demanding hike. You've spent so many years drifting that you can hardly feel your muscles. Your inner discipline has greatly diminished.

What happened to the fun you were having? Where did those people go who were coasting along beside you? How did you end up so alone? You begin searching the horizon for an answer. You call out: Is anyone there who can help me? At first you hear nothing and feel extraordinary despair. Eventually you see a small ray of light illuminating a different path through the woods. You can't see where it goes and you're too afraid to take it.

After days and nights of paralyzing fear, you decide the unknown path must be better than where you are. You step towards the light. This uphill trail requires physical strength that you didn't know you had. But as you take each unsteady step, you slowly realize that someone or something is guiding and comforting you.

After an intense climb that pushes you to face all you've ever feared, you find yourself standing at the summit, in the place you always wanted to find but thought was impossible.

You take a deep breath and enjoy the stunning view – until you notice that thousands of struggling souls are still lost in the trees below the summit, crying for help. Without hesitation, you reach your hand down to help. You remember what joy felt like.

When a storm moves in, you build the shelter that saves lives. When you see tragedy, you bring healing grace to it. When you find yourself in the dark, you seek the stars because you know they exist. You understand that after the darkest night the sun does indeed rise again.

You're absolutely sure now that something guides you. You think back to those days of being terrified and alone in the darkness, and you realize that a loving force was always with you

– even when you ignored it. When you landed in the dirt, somehow you always stood up again.

You fully allow this loving force to shine through you now, to enlighten others. When you look down at the old path far below and see lost souls wandering in the shadows, you feel only compassion. You reach out to help.

You realize that the "you," the personality, the ego, you worked so hard to sustain in your early years is slipping away. Only this inner light, this awesome love, remains.

Was it worth the effort? You realize now that was never the question. The only question was: When will you make the effort?

Everyone makes it eventually. It's only a matter of how long we linger in the shadows before we reach for the light.

Because the light calls everyone. And the light is stronger than the dark. Whatever words you put to it, you eventually realize that there's so much divine intervention in the climb and that the darkest moments are the greatest awakenings, and that without the dark, you wouldn't seek the light.

So you would never trade where you are now for anything. Because you never understand the beauty of the climb until you've stepped into the light. And here is better than anywhere. And that's all that's ever mattered.

Getting a New Prescription for Your Divine Lens

Do you see the shimmer of light in every moment, the possibility inside of each spoken word, the gift in every challenge? Do you see how your pain is a perfect opportunity to awaken to your higher self? Do you understand that self doubt is a temporary blindness caused by the distorted view of your ego lens blocking out the light?

If not, it may be time for a new divine lens prescription. With your divine lens in place, your view of divine order is restored. You find light in darkness and love where you once felt pain.

Whenever you remove your divine lens and replace it with the ego lens, you'll wonder where all the darkness came from. When did unrelenting pain arrive on your doorstep? "Why do good people suffer needlessly in our meaningless world?" you'll ask.

You're not alone in this distorted view. Many others, especially those in power, are aligned with this dark view. They see tragedy everywhere and believe hatred is necessary - because someone is always to blame.

When you wear this dark lens, you feel righteous, judgmental and superior. But this distorted viewpoint does not empower you. It encourages you to give up. You've failed before, says the ego, why bother now?

And for a little while you'll try to forget you have a soul. You'll fall into the temporary spell of soul-less living and your ego will have a party. When you wake in the morning bruised and beaten, you'll search for a better view. You'll seek the light because you'll have fallen so far into the darkness that it scared you.

As you pick up your other lens, the one you left buried in the drawer of your unconsciousness, you may be leery of the light you unexpectedly see inside of everything. How can this possibly be true, you'll ask. How can there be so much light and love where before I saw none? Am I being foolish now?

You may drop your divine lens back into the drawer. Save it for another day. But one day you will find yourself alone, heart broken, divorced, broke, addicted, grief stricken or depressed.

You'll search for those brighter lenses again to ease your pain. This time you'll smile when you see light in every dark corner. You'll feel gratitude for the ones who hurt you badly, because that pain pushed you to seek the light.

Trying again is the world

Kindness is everything. Getting back up is all that matters. **Trying again is the world.** Looking back you'll see the choices you could have made. Make them now. The road less traveled you could have taken. Take it now...

Take a tiny step into hope. It's a small clearing – mostly a break in the storm. You're not sure. Go. Put your feet on the path. Break it all wide open.

You've already lost so much here. And you're still standing. That's all that matters. Dust yourself off. The storm actually saved you. You thought it would destroy you. Nothing will ever destroy you.

Feel that searing heartbreak. Let it rise up from your chest and skim across the water like a manta ray – horrifying and beautiful - happy to be set free.

Take a stand at the front of the room. Your story needs to be told. Forgive the part of you that took a wrong path. It was a misguided attempt to find heaven – the divine realms from which you came. Every lost step was you trying to reclaim the love that flows so fiercely in the next realm. All mistakes are forgiven in the end.

Nothing is the same here in this density. Everything takes effort. Trying to recreate heaven on earth has caused you grief. You're here to feel everything and save everyone – to share your wisdom – fearlessly.

Say: "I *will* do what is hard, what is required of me, the thing I fear - because I know it will save someone, lift someone out of pain, comfort a mother, brother, sister, friend. *It will save me.*"

Courage is born in your heart and not your mind. Use it. Or it dies in your heart - a rosebud never opened, a bird with no song, a light never shared. You can't see it now. But courage is everything. And trying again is the world...

A Day In The Life: Stepping Into The Divine Lens View of Everyday Life

When we're in the routine of everyday life, we get bogged down in drudgery and forget to reach for the divine view of each moment. We get lost in details. This is the unconsciousness caused by routine life. And life here in the physical world is still mostly built on routine.

Yet your divine lens is always ready to reveal a more enlightened perspective. If you fully believed that each instant of your day was rich with divine order, with gifts and lessons all for your highest good, how might you react differently to daily annoyances? Seeking the divinity in everything fills you with light and inspires your routine chores – transforming them into little miracles.

Some examples: **Your child is crying in a crowded public place and you feel embarrassed and angry. Your ego mind** tells you to control or punish because you're embarrassed. Yet hidden beneath this annoyance is a gift of opportunity. You can choose to see a child needing love rather than a child misbehaving. This shift of perspective opens your heart and gives you instant access to more choices in your behavior. You can choose to feel compassion in spite of embarrassment. Seeing your child's tantrum as an opportunity to find love changes the behavior. Your child feels recognized. Your higher self takes over and calms you down. Tension dissipates and you've gracefully risen above your anger.

Imagine you're at work and you receive a very nasty email from a co-worker. Your ego tells you their facts are wrong and you need to defend yourself by illuminating the errors in their complaint. While your ego points out the many flaws of your co-worker – somewhere deep inside, your divine self is also speaking up: "Stop. Breathe. Open your heart. See the insecurity, fear and frustration of your co-worker. Respond with something helpful from your soul's wisdom that gets at the core of what they're really asking for – which is usually respect. This will create a better solution for everyone in the long run."

Is your nasty co-worker really looking for approval and respect? Of course they are. Everyone is always looking for that – especially in the work place. If this person felt respected or appreciated for the work they do, they wouldn't be on the attack. How might you help? How might you offer an empowering response that helps them feel better about who they are in the workplace? This is how your soul views the situation.

Only when everyone feels honored and empowered will a workplace thrive. Think of this moment (before you respond to the nasty email) as a moment of choice for your soul and for the future of the company. Responding with kindness might create a ripple effect that eventually changes the energy and future success of this business.

Take a breath, ask for guidance, and begin writing from your inner wisdom. YOU are the teacher here, the one carrying the light into this situation. As you bring others into the light, you heal yourself.

You've already tried all of the possible ego responses before and where have they gotten you? Have they created a loving home and passionate, joyful relationships at work? Would you consider taking a breath now, pausing the ego reaction, asking for guidance and asking to view this situation differently - through your divine lens?

See this person standing before you as a struggling soul on a journey (just like you) doing the best they can within their level of awareness. Try to see the pain and hurt that they carry. Can you see how they look to you for love and guidance even though their words and actions deny this? Can you see this soul as a divine being starved for love and healing? Once you shift into that perspective, everything changes; your mind quiets, your heart opens, your energy shifts away from fear and you step into wisdom.

In one moment of awareness, you can tap into your divinity, reach out to another soul, offer them a hand, and pull them out of fear. Others have done this for you. Now it's your turn to offer this gift. Reacting from wisdom rather than ego breaks a negative pattern within yourself that you're ready to release.

From this moment forward, you're the teacher, the light carrier capable of shifting everyone to a new level of consciousness, capable of enlightening work and family interactions and bringing everyone into love. What will you say now? How is this different from your old reactions?

Whatever problems you're facing in the external world, your solutions lie in the inner world. When you can't pay bills, your ego reveals a future of escalating financial failure that leads to losing everything. But when you grasp desperately for solutions out of fear, you become the angry victim, the one who works harder than everyone else and never thrives. Good solutions can't be found from this perspective.

Yet your higher self says: You're capable of creating abundance and comfort by aligning your work with your true gifts, by making a passionate commitment to a career that empowers you and fulfills your greatest potential. Each time you've chosen work for security's sake, it has eventually led you to this financial abyss.

Taking one step today to explore a new career might open doors you could never imagine. Tweaking the career you already have and bringing it to a greater level of fulfillment could also change everything. It's time to consider new possibilities that have been buried inside of you - stuffed away under layers of fear and self-doubt. This is the moment to pick up the phone and make that call, to research a new business, to email your friend who said you might be a good fit in their new company.

It's time to reach for your divine lens and acknowledge your soul's perspective. What is your soul asking of you in this moment? Listen to the whisper within, the answer that dissipates fear and leaves you empowered and inspired. Trust your wisdom and take steps in a new direction.

18

PAIN IS YOUR FUEL

Your perfectly painful childhood

When we use our divine lens to see what lies beyond the surface, we realize that everyone experiences pain throughout life and especially during childhood – whether we felt unloved, inadequate, rejected, unlovable, impoverished, or abused. We all grow up hungry – in one way or another. This hunger creates our desire to evolve.

You chose to be born into a family with the perfect dysfunctional challenges to push you in exactly the way you needed to be pushed, to help you break negative patterns you may have carried for lifetimes. The ego says this isn't true; that many people had it better than you and many people had it worse. Both statements are correct. But everyone's childhood was perfectly designed for their highest good.

Look deeply and you'll see the soul story behind everyone's beautiful and terrible life. Your friend who was raised by brilliant, successful parents struggled with crippling self-doubt because she felt unworthy compared to family members. Confidence is the lesson this soul came to learn in this lifetime.

Your co-worker, who was raised in foster homes and abused as a child, struggled to find the grace in each moment of pain, to embrace her wisdom in order to thrive. She found courage because it was her only option. It was her soul's mission to find light in the midst of darkness.

Each child is here to forge his or her own unique path. The more powerful the parents – the greater the child struggles to find true self. If you were born into great wealth and privilege, you'll struggle to find what really matters amidst the temptations of self-indulgence and addictions. These lessons are designed perfectly for your highest good. If you were born into great poverty and hardship, your soul is here to find brilliance and new solutions, to think beyond limitations. This is the mission you chose and the gifts you carry within you.

When you view your childhood from the ego lens, you may see a tragic story of injustice where you're a victim. The ego mind will tell you that because of your suffering you have a right to be angry, desperate, afraid or cruel. You may spend much of your life with this paralyzing viewpoint until you hit a crisis.

When your pain is great enough, you may finally choose to shift into your divine perspective. You'll realize how perfectly you chose your childhood and those relationships so that you could find your divinity, look beyond the surface, and embrace the wisdom of your soul.

This is your soul story, and it's the only perspective that matters. Your ego tells you otherwise. But your soul story is the true one and it empowers you. It's the viewpoint you'll realize at the moment of your final breath.

To gain a new perspective on your life, write two different versions of your childhood - each with the same players and circumstances. In the ego story, you're the helpless victim without a choice to make things better. In your soul story, change your inner perceptions to find love and miracles in each painful moment. Use these moments of wisdom to rewrite your history and change your choices for the better, finding courage whenever you faced fear. Now you see who you came here to be. This is your new story and your new point of view moving forward.

Ask yourself which version of the story makes me feel open-hearted, forgiving and empowered? Which version leaves me feeling hopeless? You get to choose your lens; the soul's view or the ego's view. Choose wisely. Your happiness and future direction depend on which lens you choose – not on the circumstances of your life.

We want to believe that everything lasts. We last. Our loved ones last. That what we feel today is forever. But it's more like water. Waves upon waves of change and uncertainty shifting around us causing us to lose our footing – to go under and drink the salty brine and come up gasping for air - unsure of who we are. Where we are. Or if we're alone.

We instinctively search for a horizon. A landing place. Safety. Anywhere. Until we find something solid to gaze upon and we feel secure again. Certain nothing will change. **But we're still standing in the ocean.** The next wave is always bigger and knocks us over because we had our back to it.

We learn. We open our arms wide and embrace the waves. Laugh as they lift us higher in the air to reveal the greater view - the bigger picture. Hungrily we drink in that vast landscape noting the lighthouse we never saw before, the gull resting calmly on nothing halfway out to nowhere, and the long glistening white fish jumping high above the wave teasing us with its mystery.

We marvel at beauty. Knowing that something creates this – if not the gull itself. If not the water itself. A divine poet arranges the details. But who and how? We write books about this unknowingness, create careers analyzing it, build damns and concrete roads and bridges and still the water swirls around us mysteriously because we are amidst the living sea.

We *are* the living sea. That sea is in us; it courses through our veins; beats in our hearts. Just when we think we've discovered everything, that no one has ever known as much...

A wave rolls towards us from nowhere and we are teetering terrified above everything in the rush of changing water. We surrender once again to the power of the grand poet - as we're pushed back to the ground by the force of the wave – our limbs dancing madly out of control, our heads brushing painfully against the sand, twisting and turning with abandon - until the wave releases us again. We struggle to our feet gasping – taking in raw sobbing breaths. Calling out to our friends whom we may have lost in the crushing waves.

Someday we *do* arrive on the beach through no efforts of our own. Then we realize we had choices in how we rode those waves. There are others who floated above them and some who fought and loss and drowned beneath them, and many who struggled endlessly when they only needed to surrender to the ride, rest their heads upon the salty brine - not trying to stand where it was impossible to stand.

And we see that we exhausted ourselves when we fought it, and that it would have been wiser to relax, surrender, laugh and even reach towards someone else who was going under.

We see then that all souls make it to shore one day or another – one way or another. And that all that ever mattered was how we rode the lovely waves. And if we brought someone along with us to the vast white shore.

Using childhood pain as fuel for doing meaningful work

Peter was a 40-year-old computer programmer who hated his job and had a passion for race-car driving. He spent so much time at the race-track that his marriage was in trouble. His doctor prescribed anti-depressants and sent him to me for career counseling. Peter's story was unforgettable.

One night when Peter was 13, his 16-year-old sister woke him up. "Mom and dad have gone out. Get in the back seat of the car and shut up," she whispered. "We're going for a ride."

Peter followed her into the family car and fell asleep in the back seat. He woke up hours later in the darkness, in a ditch, unable to find his sister. She was pinned under the car and died instantly. That moment changed his life forever. His parents divorced, his father became an alcoholic, and "no one ever spoke about the accident. In fact, no one ever spoke at all," he remembered. Peter became an outcast in high school and learned to bottle up his feelings. "Have a stiff upper lip and carry on," was his father's only advice.

As my client, he explored this memory and realized that each time he raced a car at 80 miles an hour around a race track he was healing a childhood wound. He was reliving and re-programming the event that had destroyed his childhood. He was taking control of his greatest pain - the loss of his sister and family. He also recognized that teaching someone else how to navigate a speeding car was a profoundly healing experience for him.

By facing his pain, Peter gave himself permission to pursue a career as a race car driving instructor and a race car service and repair shop owner. By honestly sharing his insights with his wife and daughter, he rallied their support for his new direction. He found renewed intimacy in his marriage, and gave himself permission to pursue work that he loved.

This brings me to the most powerful truth I know about meaningful work: Your pain is your greatest ally for finding work you love. Consider that you chose (consciously or unconsciously) every job you've had in your lifetime because it was healing you.

Hundreds of my clients have proven this to be true. From observing their experiences and studying the biographies of successful people, I am 100% SURE that our pain guides us to our true work; and that our true work heals our greatest pain.

How? Our work heals us by letting us offer to the world exactly what we need to heal ourselves. By facing our pain, we turn it into energy. It becomes our ally and moves us forward. Ask yourself what pain needs healing now? Let that answer guide you to work you love.

Here's the secret: The more pain you feel, the more energy you have to launch your new career. See the pain as fuel - not as something that stops you from moving forward.

In my 20s, I enjoyed a career as a mountaineering instructor for Colorado Outward Bound School. I loved empowering people and inspiring them to overcome their fears. Throughout my own childhood (as a woman growing up in the south in the 50s), I felt afraid and un-empowered. This work of empowering others felt very meaningful to me; it was healing my childhood wounds. And I was having great fun!

I was married to a fellow mountaineer whom I adored, and our happy life was filled with climbing adventures and mountaineering trips.

My husband had stomach problems but was told by a couple doctors that it was nothing more than a nervous stomach or the beginnings of an ulcer. By the time we got a proper diagnosis of colon cancer, the doctors gave Paul two weeks to live.

Paul died one year later. From that moment on, I couldn't climb or teach mountaineering anymore. My life changed, and my work changed. I went back to school to study journalism and spent years working as a newspaper reporter (health writer), magazine editor (writing about natural health), and a VP of Content for natural health websites. I was passionate about writing stories that helped people prevent disease and live healthy lives. I was healing my own pain with each story.

As my awareness evolved through spiritual work, I became passionate about helping everyone see their greatness, their indestructible soul, and the mission they came to accomplish. I allowed my intuition to flow through untethered and used it to help others. I learned to focus on the client's luminous spirit, the great potential they came to fulfill in this lifetime, and the beauty of their pain story - so perfectly designed to help them evolve. This is the work I do today.

When you're unhappy in your career, it's time to face your greatest ally - your pain. The pain you're feeling deep inside of you is like a beacon calling for your attention. It's telling you what you need to know so your life can move forward.

Your pain needs to be recognized, listened to, and turned into fuel to move your life forward.

How do you turn your pain into fuel? First by recognizing what your greatest pain is, and then by recognizing how to heal that pain through your work.

Your career then becomes a powerful platform for healing you and healing others. Remember, the more pain you have, the more fuel you have. Consider your pain to be your greatest blessing and move forward.

From My Soul to Yours: The Play's the Thing

There's no joy without pain – no pain without joy – when all is said and done. We have to love the play for what it is – a textbook of mastery for our divine evolution.

Of course, like you, I long to step away from the pain and live in the bliss – meditating on my porch while a summer breeze stirs my heart and I cry from the beauty of a tree in the morning sun; the perfect dance of light and dark; the brilliance of a morning dove's sweet song; the song that wakes us up from the bliss of higher realms.

In a moment of sudden panic at the airport, I hold my daughter forever, kiss her lovely forehead and never let her go. I stop her from walking towards the gate away from me. Then, like mothers do, I blow her a kiss good-bye as she disappears from view. She too needs to see the beauty and the horror side by side. We all must sip from this potent brew or there's no need to be here. It's the play and the play's the thing.

And when you take your final bow, it matters how honestly you spoke your lines, how bravely you faced the audience; if you played your role with every ounce of heart you could muster. It matters how true your words rang out into the night - filling the audience with hope, sorrow and understanding; your poetry drifting into a moonlit sky.

But the play's the thing. And it gets me out of bed. It's the thing that holds us together waiting for the divine reveal. We hope for one word of unbroken truth to fall into our hearts and touch us so deeply that for a brief instant we remember who we are and leap to our feet shouting *"Bravo!!"* For that one moment, we see the perfection of horror and beauty. We understand the play of light and shadow; and it illuminates us.

Only at the final curtain call can we say it was terrible and wonderful and that we're glad we came – that the story was worth it. And the script was brilliant.

Be the player on the stage we can't forget. Pull the naked truth from your heart and lay it on the stage for all to see. Speak your untarnished wisdom that wakes us up for a brief instant of shared illumination. *Because you are divine and nothing can stop you...*

When everything is stripped away, who's left inside? Your divine self. Your soul. **When you've lost everything, what have you found?** Your divinity.

Take the opening. Take the chance. You've nothing else to lose. All obstacles, belongings, and attachments have been removed for your highest good; to open your heart, break patterns, erase fear, and quiet the ego mind that's been obsessed with winning.

Pain quiets the personality that hides our true selves from the world. When it all slips away, take a breath. Just one breath connects you to your divinity, to your divine perspective.

Say this sentence out loud: Show me my divine perspective, the lesson of my pain, the gift in this moment, and my next step. One breath, one sentence spoken out loud, and everything is revealed. Now you're ready for your next level of evolution, the next phase of your journey. Today you're being asked to release the old, step away from drudgery, throw open the window and kiss the unknown dawn that awaits.

You're being asked to grow, to love what you fear, to embrace pain as your greatest gift. Will you consider this? Can you pray: "Help me see this differently. Pull me out of ego. Wrap me in love and understanding."

You're not weak or too sensitive. There's nothing wrong with you. You're a divine being who came here with a plan. You may have lost your way but that's what happens in this dense realm. None of your past matters. What you have is today. And today is your choice.

All that matters is finding your way through the fog, reaching for divinity, seeking inspired purpose, and refusing to live by the rules that others have determined for your life.

Your soul is in charge, always. Your personality is only the shell you chose, the costume you wear. Your soul opens every door, pours love on every wound, sees beauty in every misstep. Your soul realizes this is simply the journey you chose to take on your way to higher consciousness.

Everything you touch in this physical world is infused with love; Your desk, your jeans, your drinking glass all contain an energy, a vibration of consciousness capable of assisting you in your awakening. Have respect for the unseen consciousness that exists everywhere within and without you.

You didn't come here to waste time and indulge in your pain. You have everything you need in the higher realms. You chose this density, this layer of darkness and fog, so you could surprise yourself, awaken and remember everything, recognize your opponent as the teacher, see your heartbreak as wisdom arriving, and realize that grief calls everyone to the divine.

Every task you perform here, every job you undertake, is calling you to your soul's true work. **Nothing is meant to be** drudgery, torture, or work for work's sake -even though many choose to see it this way. Our lives are meant to elevate, inspire, heal and awaken.

Where were you when your last lesson broke you open? Do you remember? Did you pout and blame? Or did you swing the doors of your heart wide open and call out for guidance?

Did you attack those who asked you to grow? If so, this was your ego-self acting out, your empty personality disconnected from soul; The hungry ghost inside of you.

It's time to make amends. You get to choose again. You can open your arms with gratitude, laugh instead of cower in fear, and move through the fog into the light – the light that was always there.

All you can hope for is to take the first step and reach for a sweeter answer. Everything will change in an instant of making a new choice. Because everything you feared is then revealed as nothing but illusion. All that matters is your courageous heart. That's where the light lives. That's your essence and now you can see it.

In the end, you'll see your loved ones standing in the light beside you. "You did it!" they'll cry as they hold you. You'll realize that you never truly understood there was something important to do. You forgot there was a plan you agreed to.

Yet when life's disappointments drained you, and heartbreak sucked your breath away, you finally stood up. Not fully remembering why or how, you reached for the light in that painful moment. You loved it more than you loved the darkness. And in spite of everything, you found your courage.

Consider the possibility that all of your pain – every wound you've ever experienced, from loss to illness to disappointment – was exactly what you needed and chose in order to arrive at this point in your life which is exactly where you're supposed to be.

Imagine that your soul chose to experience loss to open your heart and strengthen your connection to the divine – to push you onto your true path and inspire you to accomplish your soul's greatest mission.

Your greatest work offers to the world what you wish had been offered to you in your moment of greatest pain. Grief brings a clarity and focus to your life's purpose that gives you a powerful advantage in everything you do. Pain of any kind will drive you to see beyond the surface and embrace a divine lens perspective in every area of your life.

Let me tell you a story...

I'm constantly amazed at how everyone has a story of loss. And how for too many people that grief has poisoned their lives in subtle ways.

Recently, on the way to teach a grief-shifting workshop at a spiritual retreat center on the east coast, my shuttle driver (we'll call him Joe) told me he spent 10 years angry at God and angry at his family for his father's sudden traumatic death.

His pain destroyed his marriage, career and health. One day he was considering ending his life when he felt his departed father's presence. The overwhelming love and grace he felt from his father – who had been tragically murdered – convinced Joe that he was living in a state of anger and blame while his departed father was living in a state of pure love. Joe knew he needed to change his life and start again. He began his journey of searching for a new spiritual perspective outside of church and religion.

Today he studies with people like the psychic James Van Praagh, and is becoming a healer and a medium. He says he realizes now that there were soul agreements in place - including an agreement to learn through the pain of loss - which he resisted for years because of anger.

And he talks to his departed dad everyday now for guidance and healing. This brings him great comfort.

That's the same story as mine and the same path I took after my husband's death in 1980.

Whatever your pain story is, shifting into your divine lens will reveal a new way forward, illuminate your pain as fuel, clear the confusion and open your heart.

19

Joy and Gratitude

How Gratitude Shifts Us Into the Divine Lens Perspective

From one moment to the next, we can shift from despair to enlightenment, from grief to gratitude, from terror to love. This is our gift as humans; the ability to choose the way we view and thus live our lives - no matter our circumstances. Our perception of challenge is never constant. It's always shifting. This is how we learn. Free will is essential to our evolution.

If you had incarnated into this dense realm fully remembering that you're soul on a mission to evolve consciousness, you wouldn't learn anything here. It would be like playing monopoly but starting out already owning all the hotels and properties. You'd feel nothing. There wouldn't be joy, surprise, excitement, or disappointment. There would be no point to the game and nothing learned.

We come here for one reason: to evolve and help others evolve. We arrive ready for the adventure of learning, of new experiences. Just as we enroll in the university for the adventure of learning, new experiences, and friendship, we enroll in earth school.

You signed up for your coursework before you arrived here, carefully choosing the exact lessons and gifts that would help you evolve in the way you needed to and would push you to advance to your next level.

At certain points, all of us become angry, disappointed or depressed over the exact lessons we come here to master. But we can shift our consciousness from anger and fear to love and gratitude no matter what we're facing. Then we step into the grace and peace of our soul's wisdom. This choice once made becomes a lifetime pattern that will serve us at every challenge.

We may also choose to exit the lifetime through suicide or by sabotaging our physical health but if we haven't accomplished our soul's mission we'll still need to do so during another lifetime. When we cross over through intentional death, our life review reveals the life choices we made and could have made. We feel the ramifications of each choice and how it affected our loved ones. Great learning occurs in this moment of ultimate realization.

We see then the choices we could have made to change our lives for the better. We're shown the love that was given to us that we might've denied. And we see the life we originally came here to create. All of this spurs soul growth – along with a determination to try again and accomplish more.

We may then choose to start over - facing the same challenges as last time and determined to reverse the pain we caused our loved ones. Or we might choose to remain in the divine realms – to do our work from there.

If you feel resistant to the idea of viewing your life in a new way, take a deep breath, quiet your mind, and ask for a new perspective on your pain. This request is always answered. One moment of gratitude is capable of pulling you into your soul's wisdom.

Say: I'm grateful for the lessons because I know I chose them to help me become my best self. I trust that if I embrace this pain with love and wisdom, I'll step into my divinity, and experience the grace that awaits me.

How Joy Trumps Everything - Including Pain

We come to this realm to experience the tastes, smells, passions, and enormous beauty of the physical world. We use contrast to push us to evolve. Fear forces us to choose love. Despair makes us reach for hope. Winter's quiet contemplation prepares us for the new growth of spring awakening.

Your darkest despair carries a glimmer of light that will change everything – if you reach for it. In your moment of greatest fear, there's a voice of pure love singing a new song - if you listen to it.

It's your choice and yours alone to pull yourself through the storm. One moment of shared laughter or unrestrained joy shatters pain into a million pieces of light. When you look into someone's eyes to realize you've always known them, you remember your divinity. When a butterfly emerges from nowhere to land on your shoulder, you realize you're not alone. This is the gift of human experience.

You're in it for the beauty, the awe of an unexpected moment. But you must choose the joy. In spite of everything you've been through, miracles occur everyday just for you – during your daily walk, in your random conversation with a stranger, and in the sudden brush of a fresh breeze against your skin.

When your soul is ready, and you've learned what you came for, you'll be pulled into the highest realms where the light is brighter than here and the sounds are more ecstatic than you've known before. But today you're here for the joy of taking another breath.

Joy is your natural state. Your divine lens view pulls back the veil to reveal the perpetual light, love, and beauty that's always working for your highest good.

Experience this enlightened view and it will break your heart wide open with joy. Pick up your divine lens and allow a new perspective to inspire your mundane life; you'll see that all is well and there exists a higher purpose to your journey.

It's this higher purpose that keeps us going as we navigate this dense realm, accomplish daily tasks and survive. Yet within this daily grind, we often forget our divinity and shut out our view of divine order. Instead we focus on details and the meaningless activities that fill our lives with drudgery. This focus on empty details blocks our joy. We briefly remember this inner joy when we hold a new baby, walk in nature or fall in love.

Yet you've evolved enough now that you're capable of navigating this dense energy while also experiencing your divine self, your bliss, and remembering the higher purpose of your life. When challenges occur, when you lose a loved one, a job, or face financial hardship, you're being pushed to see divine order even as you mourn a loss or struggle to build a new career. One breath, one moment of silent meditation or a request for guidance opens your channel to divine wisdom.

You've accomplished so much already and in a relatively short time. But now your evolution has reached a tipping point and your growth curve has steepened. You're awakening into the awareness that this physical world is your creation, your university of divinity.

Take notice of the brief moment before you react in pain, fear or anger. Listen for the whisper of your soul. This subtle inner voice, like a sudden breeze against your skin or a tingle up your spine, urges you to seek guidance, to step into higher consciousness and face this moment with awareness of your divinity.

When you listen to the whisper, your soul's wisdom speaks up. It says: I will rise above my pain with grace and love - knowing that I'm not alone, that love surrounds me, and that when I ask for guidance I'm lifted into the light where my next step is fully revealed.

Doing this once changes everything. It breaks a pattern. Now you know you can shift your perspective. You've begun your awakening and nothing can stop the process. Not even your ego.

This seedling of wisdom will slowly blossom in your heart in spite of your pain, illuminating moments of joy when you least expect them. You'll discover that you're never a victim to anyone or anything.

You'll navigate this earthly realm with both sides of your brain activated; your ego mind will organize the details while your higher self illuminates the greater purpose.

20

RETURN TO SACRED SELF

From My Soul to Yours: Doubt is Easy...

My pain is the same as everyone's. My fear is shared by all.

There is no dark night of the soul I can have that you haven't had. We share this journey. We joined our souls long ago. We dove in. We agreed. We swim beside each other now. Forgetting. Fighting the flow. Resisting wisdom.

Why?

Because doubt is easy. Fear is ordinary. We give up. A million times. A billion times...

But here's the thing. We hit the dirt but we always rise again. We reach for light after days of pacing in the dark. We long to feel love. We long to help. **We want life. We breathe. We choose.**

Never doubt that you have the gift. Never doubt that you walk in grace. **Never doubt that every rising up and falling down is perfect** - meant to be - fuel for the journey of your soul.

You're right on schedule. Relax. **Trust your gut.** You're learning what you must.

Someday when your heart is ripped open, your head thrown back in awe, and you're gasping at the light – you'll see the purpose of your whole crazy story. You'll know it was good. All good...

This exact moment is very good. All good. Trust it...

Choose love. Choose what you love.

Because doubt is easy. Fear is ordinary.

Whether it appears so or not, all souls on earth are cooperating in divine agreement for everyone's highest evolutionary good. You agreed to come here to evolve your soul and to help others in your soul family. You may have suffered greatly in your lifetime journey. But this was all agreed to ahead of time for your highest good.

It may appear that some people have everything they desire, or they seem untouched by hardship. Rest assured they're experiencing exactly what you're experiencing - just wrapped in a different package. The lessons are the same for all of us no matter how things appear on the surface.

Your divine lens provides a way to see beyond the surface. It illuminates the deeper story in the soul journey of those you love and those you condemn. Wearing your powerful divine lens, you see divinity in everything, within each spoken word and painful moment. It reveals the hidden agreements of soul upon soul.

You may be highly intelligent. But true intelligence is the wisdom to see beyond the surface, to know the essence of things. You may consider yourself inferior or superior. But these are meaningless terms that only weigh you down with confusion. They make you doubt who you are and why you came here.

Through your divine lens, you see the perfection in every heartbreak and the wisdom within every life story – especially your own. Your ego lens distortion convinces you that some people are good and others are bad. Viewing the world in this way is a side-effect of ego - which is incapable of seeing beyond the surface. The ego is bereft of wisdom, compassion and insight.

Shift into your divine lens view right now. Close your eyes. Take a deep breath. Quiet the mind. Open the heart. Ask for guidance. Surrender what you know...

Every moment of your day is a new beginning. One fear-based judgmental action is erased by a moment of wisdom. When we trust our divine guides, they help us quiet the ego mind; this allows our heart to become the force of light that it was designed to be. Love is the radiant light that slices through ignorance to reveal the divine order of each moment.

So many untapped gifts abound within you that when you arrive at the end of your journey and the ego lens is finally ripped away, you'll stand in awe at the brilliance and perfection of each moment of your life. The astounding gifts you brought to the lifetime will leave you stunned; you'll realize you could have changed the world.

We don't come here to be perfect. We come here to learn.

We come for the experience of soul expansion, growth, and consciousness evolution. If those terms seem foreign to you, if they don't speak to your pain, ask yourself: Can I remember one moment when I felt awe at something beyond logic, beyond description, something that took my breath away and for a brief instant held me in deepest contentment - knowing all is well?

If you remember one moment like this, one second, then you know how you'll feel at the end when you cross the veil and view your life to see the soul lessons. You can choose to view your life this way today, even as you doubt yourself, you can look within to know your soul's story.

The power of your asking

Great love lives within you and your soul has taken gracious care to design this moment of heartbreak perfectly for your evolution. The joy of your un-birthed wisdom is waiting to be set free.

All of this light and possibility shimmers within even when you fall to your knees in despair or pound your fist with anger. Sacred light shines within your heart, bright as gold, sharp as a sword, and true as the sun. Nothing ever diminishes it not even when you deny your soul's wisdom and fail to see beyond one moment of suffering.

Hidden in the heart of your cynicism is the truth you're not speaking, the pain you're not embracing: You long for love. Absolute love. Your misplaced homesickness for the divine has caused you deep misery. You feel stranded, ripped from the vast endless ocean of unconditional love that you once knew in the higher dimensions.

How did you arrive on this earthly shore gasping for air? You swam here, poured your enormous spirit into a brief and imperfect body and a flawed personality. Your soul did this to create the exact circumstances you now find yourself in.

When you first arrived, you remembered that nothing could ever damage your essence; the diamond of your indestructible soul. You longed to expand consciousness, spread your wings, pour light into darkness and transform everyone with love. You carried that love with you when you jumped into this dense realm - where you now lay abandoned on the beach of your despair.

Remember this: The sand will slap you awake and scrape skin from your bones until you clear your mind and open your heart again. It doesn't matter what you've been through or how damaged you feel. When your head clears, you'll see the beauty of your devastating loss and the gift it offers – a reminder of your divine essence, your indestructible heart, and the enormous love you came here to share. All losses disappear in the end. Someday you'll remember this.

But today perhaps you only feel the rough sand against your face and grieve the memory of something divine you once knew. Perhaps your thoughts are dark at this moment. Your guides understand this and wait for your awakening. Your voyage must not be interfered with. But the waves of wisdom stirring within you will never stop eroding your ego and opening your eyes.

When a new tide comes, you won't be able to remember your grief and disappointment. The moment you lift your head and cry for help from something you don't even believe in, you'll find yourself cloaked in light and wisdom. The moment you seek a new answer, love arrives and changes everything.

My ego story is terribly sad; I was abused, abandoned and grief stricken. I failed at many things. I was too sensitive, never perfect, and hardly lovable.

Yet my soul story is filled with light: There were angels in my darkest moments. Spirits warned me of danger and pushed me into the light when I was young.

Those whom I grieved showed up to heal me - again and again. Whenever I lifted my eyes from the pain they were standing there in the light. I felt them reaching through my grief. I saw them vividly in dreams.

Whenever I asked for divine inspiration, it always arrived - looking different from what I expected but delivering me into the light nonetheless. When I didn't demand that life turn out my way, but instead surrendered to the lesson, asking only for grace and wisdom - events conspired in my favor and for my highest good. I have no regrets. I've been pushed to learn exactly what I came here to learn and rewarded abundantly for every effort I made to reach for the grace hidden inside of a painful moment.

I now understand the love that surrounded me especially when I felt abandoned and broken hearted. I acknowledge the unstoppable truth that poured through my heart once I learned to quiet my mind. I realize now that the passion, the intensity I've always held inside was my gift and never my flaw - though I often believed it was my terrible weakness.

The moments I thought were easy and hoped would last forever did not serve my highest good. They were brief because I didn't come here to sleep or waste time. I planned well for the trip, choosing the perfect body type and personality for the job (even though these things were often a source of shame).

I designed the excruciating self doubt and intellectual awkwardness that would eventually force me to share my wisdom fearlessly - because I had learned too well the price of remaining silent, the price of pleasing others, and the bankruptcy of living for approval from anyone - other than my higher self.

I recognize now that my over-active right brain and under-developed left-brain forced me to find alternative ways to navigate. This intuitive compass was my gift, grand and luminous, that delivered me into a world of endless possibility and boundless optimism.

Because I couldn't see the logic of not jumping off the cliff and instead felt, with all my heart, that the jump must be made, I

took the leap; it was the leap that changed everything and brought me into the glory of a luminous world that lives within everyone and everything.

And once I'd made that leap it became so easy to do it again, and again, whenever I found myself in a corner and couldn't see the light. I had discovered that light lives in the leap. And love awaits the courageous act. And now nothing could ever keep me from the leap or dampen my courage. What a gift this was and I am still so grateful. It is the best truth I ever learned and worth every bruise I ever suffered.

Without the leap we don't understand a thing. We think the glory is in the withholding, the caution, politeness, acceptance and boundaries. But none of those places hold truth. And none of them teach us to fly.

Caution is a weighted thing and it puts you on the bench to watch the game or keeps you seated nervously on the cliff's edge viewing everything you fear below, counting all the reasons that a leap would ruin you, explaining all the ways it could go badly, telling stories of how to live with planning and steadfastness without ever being foolish. At the end of the game, you'll see that it was you being foolish.

Because everything that ever mattered lived in the leap; that one moment of taking a breath and trusting in the wind to carry you, seeing suddenly that letting go was everything – it was always the point of your existence and the reason for your story.

You always have access to your soul's wisdom and that's the great secret here, the jewel hidden in the vault, the thing you came to find but forgot along the way. You landed here eager to find the gem of your soul's truth and view your travels through the divine lens. But then you forgot everything you knew.

When others insisted that you were no more than a physical body, a personality locked into a physical world, you forgot your soul. You were taught the wrong rules of behavior and given the wrong advice. You pursued things that took you further from your wisdom, and made you conform to the rules of your tribe.

You were told to compete in a world where money is always the point of the story. You made choices in alignment with that even though it bothered you. But it was all you knew. You had forgotten the point of your adventure.

When your lover broke your heart or you didn't pass that exam or get the job, you tried hard to remember something essential. Sometimes you found it in music or in romantic love when a powerful feeling stirred within your heart and couldn't be denied.

As soon as the world rewarded your ego again, your ego lens was restored. Off you went to re-learn the rules, win the game and become the smartest in the room no matter the cost.

When the perfect job left you empty and questioning everything, or your new lover proved unworthy, you fell back into seeking the gem you first came to find. You discovered the hidden prize wasn't money or sex or pleasure. It wasn't any of the things you were holding. You almost remembered then.

What was that thing you were looking for?

One day your inner longing became too great and you broke open. You awakened and remembered the purpose of your existence, the reason for your life. You felt schizophrenic. One day you'd know that everything was meant to happen and you felt fearless. The next day you'd wake in fear with a sweat-drenched pillow and unpaid bills littering the floor. Then you were certain that you were headed for a tragic ending. **Which viewpoint do you favor?** The sweat-drenched nightmares? Or the moments of clarity and purpose?

Lost Days: Why does our clarity and happiness vacillate from day to day if we're divine beings?

We all experience "lost days" when we simply can't seem to connect to anything beyond the mundane world, or beyond our pain and doubt. Yet other days are filled with light and magic, and our hearts open wide to feel the divine presence of each moment.

Many factors contribute to the density of energy here on earth. One factor is the group consciousness of all souls at each moment of every day. At times, there's tremendous collective pain amongst us due to international events. At those times, we feel the veil separating us from the higher realms as thick, heavy and impenetrable. This is caused by our collective fear, anger and blame.

During these times, focus on prayer, love, forgiveness and reaching for the light. In this way, you help shift earth consciousness back into a higher frequency. This shift into the light greatly benefits everyone – especially the suffering.

At other times, the heaviness we feel is more unique to each of us; caused by our "body chi" (or life force) becoming sluggish due to toxic foods and lack of movement. Sluggish body energy keeps us weighted down in the mundane and burdened with fear.

Remember that as long as you take a breath, you're still in the game.

AS long as you're alive, you're still in the game. You may be resting on the sidelines briefly, but you're an important player, and you're needed for the next inning. Even if you're temporarily benched (dealing with fear and self-doubt) prepare yourself to jump back in. Get up and move your body. Say a prayer for inspiration. Visualize how you'll make your next move. Show your enthusiasm to the world and everything will begin feeling better.

There's nothing worse than realizing after the game ends that you've spent your lifetime sitting on the sideline watching others give it their all – knowing you had it inside of you to run the touchdown, hit the grand slam, and yet you didn't jump back in. You sat watching and judging the efforts of others. You doubted your gifts. You exhausted yourself with worry and fear.

This is not who you came here to be. You didn't arrive on earth to sit on the sidelines. You came to be a star - someone who passionately tries and tries again, a most valuable player, and someone who makes others believe that they too could do something great to serve the world.

The players sitting on the bench don't inspire us. They never get to prove to themselves that they're gifted, worthy, and carry a perpetual light inside that's needed in this world.

How many lifetimes have you spent on the bench doubting yourself or doubting the importance of the game, the worthiness of other players, the value of succeeding, or the ecstasy of giving your everything to something?

The moment you jump in and give life everything – your heart, soul and gifts – you step into the bliss, the divine connection, the thrill of this realm. You remember why you came here and why all the hard work was worth it. That one moment of giving everything carries the juice, the love, opens your heart and pushes you into the light.

Just stand up. Move that heavy energy. Get it flowing. Call out for wisdom and love. Asking is everything and movement allows grace to flow through you.

Someday you'll see it all with wisdom. You'll understand the value of a courageous heart. You'll see how courage creates the miracle, the impossible. It changes the game.

Everything worthwhile is born of courage, courage to move forward in spite of all losses and doubt. It's the one thing you truly need on earth.

How Do I Connect to Sacred Self?

Your sacred self is always available. This inner frequency is active 24/7 and there's no static to block the reception until your mind creates it. Divine guidance is always available – whenever you quiet your mind.

A simple letting go of fear allows you to hear your inner wisdom. There's nothing more important that allowing your higher self to speak. You're one of the many light beings here or you wouldn't be reading this. You've been nurtured along for this very moment; educated in the higher realms, trained in love and courage. Divinity is on your side if you embrace the lesson in front of you.

Nothing can hurt you. No one can take away your home, your love, your life as long as you open your heart and reach for the light. Speak the words you hear in your heart and share the knowledge given to you by your higher self.

There are no beings who are any more or less magnificent than you - now that you've opened your channel to the highest realms and can access your soul's wisdom. It's not your imagination. This inner voice is your divine companion – the one who has always been standing beside you.

You have always had a spirit posse on the other side rooting for you. They know when to push and when to comfort. You still need a little pushing, but you'll get this done just as you planned.

You wouldn't have chosen to incarnate at this pivotal time if you weren't up for the job of evolution. You don't have to remember making that choice. You don't have to struggle. Just ease forward as each step is revealed. Just do the work in front of you. Truth unfolds simply and elegantly; one day at a time. When you listen to your higher self, everything gets easier.

What's coming in the future? Only sweet surrender reveals it. You're not allowed to know or growth would not occur; and it's the growth you've needed for your soul's fulfillment.

Here's all you need to know:

Light is greater than dark. Always. Love is greater than fear. Always. This simple equation foretells the future of your life and the future of humanity.

Choose your side, your words, and your actions to align with the light. Move forward into grace. You are divinely blessed and deeply loved. When you choose the fear, the darkness, you're not in alignment with the grace that abounds within and without you. You're lost in the static and unable to hear the ever-present loving guidance.

Sit in silence at least once a day or so much is missed, so many mistakes made. Doing this is easier than not doing it, because everything shifts when you're silent and have quieted the mind. You'll barely realize the grace that surrounds you when you get up from your sacred stillness and go about your day. But at the end of the day, when you review events, you'll recognize the light that illuminated your choices.

All religions have tried to teach this in different ways. The ego-based ideas of humans have corrupted so much truth that was originally channeled from the divine. Religion was meant to be a ritual of silent connection, but so much was lost in human translations.

Your body is simply the vehicle that was perfectly designed for your unique journey. Each body and personality is so unique in its personal vibration. All of this was finely tuned and planned before your lifetime began. You can trust that your body and your personality are carrying you exactly where you need to go.

The same is true of your brain. Your brain was perfectly designed for the gifts you carried into this lifetime. There are no flaws in the design of any brain or body. Each piece of you is in perfect alignment with your soul's mission and what you've come here to accomplish for humanity.

The older your soul, the greater your intent to accomplish something grand, to participate in the shift for higher consciousness. You would not be reading these words if you weren't one of these old souls who came here with a great purpose.

Yet once you arrived, you struggled like everyone else to adapt to the dense energy here, often feeling like a fish out of water. Your body and brain is the earth suit you designed for the task of getting up and fulfilling your mission.

So stand up. Brush the dust off. Take a deep breath. Begin walking. Even if you don't know where to go, take a step forward. You'll be guided each inch of the way. You already have been. So take a step and trust.

Nothing is unforgivable. Nothing is impossible. Nothing is meaningless.

You're in this now. Your soul brought you here. It takes great effort to arrive in human form and begin a new lifetime. No one sent you. No one pushed you. You asked for permission. You asked to be put into the game. You'd healed from past injuries, and you had a new and better plan. You wanted to heal everyone.

The guides approved your plan before you arrived here. You agreed to reduce your enormous soul into the tiniest of forms – an earth uniform called the human body.

Once your feet were on the ground you complained, screamed and railed against the pain of being back in this thick density, in this diminished light, in the fog of forgetfulness. Certain people sparked you to open your eyes, to remember just a little. And you did.

You reached out to anyone who shimmered. They reminded you of the beings from whence you came. You always had a choice. A choice to reach out or not. A choice to ask for help or not. By making choices for the light, you emerged. In your emerging, you remembered. You found your name, your song. You heard your soul's voice.

When you take the stage to share your gifts and you stand in alignment with your highest self - all things are revealed. Each day, even your final one, is a moment of choice, and a moment to offer healing. Your soul bears the pain and the gifts of your unique journey.

Tools for accessing the divine realms

Throughout history, we've been given many tools for accessing our divinity. These sacred tools pull us out of the ego's grip and reveal our soul's purpose. Religious rituals, such as prayer, communion and chanting, are designed to connect us to the highest realms. Yet religion goes astray when its leaders focus on sin and condemnation - rather than love. God is love. If fear overshadows the sacred we lose our connection to the divine.

We were given many other techniques such as astrology, numerology, tarot, channeling and hand analysis to help us find our way. When used with love, all of these tools can reveal our divine purpose.

I've used numerology to guide clients since 1980. This sacred technique was first shared by the mystic Pythagoras in 580 BC. when he created the number system we still use today; he also taught that each number carries an energy, or sacred meaning, that goes beyond quantity.

In Pythagoras' system, we digit the birth date down to a single number in order to reveal the soul's purpose for the lifetime. So much wisdom is revealed in these numbers that they become a gateway to higher consciousness once they're fully understood.

Our elegant universe is rich with patterns and symbols that can reveal our purpose here. These patterns exist everywhere - from numbers, to stars, to nature. We came to this realm knowing there would be many signposts along the way to guide us.

For more information about the Pythagoras number system and how to use it to reveal careers and soul agreements consult the workbook at the end of this book and read my previous books: I See Your Dream Job, I See Your Soul Mate and Bridges to Heaven: True Stories of Loved Ones on the Other Side.

21

SOUL STORIES

Every Soldier's Story

Tom's father was a hero. He'd served bravely in World War II and received medals for his courage under fire. He'd raised Tom on stories of brotherhood and triumph. He pushed Tom to be strong and fearless in all things – from school to sports. Tom excelled at everything to please his dad.

Tom believed, as his father taught him, that serving in the military was his right and responsibility. Wanting to make his father proud, he enlisted at 18 and spent several years in training and on tours of duty as he advanced through military ranks.

His final tour of duty was in Iraq. He was riding in a military vehicle with several buddies when they hit a land mine. He lost two close friends that day and nearly lost a leg. He was sent home injured in body and broken in soul.

At home, he couldn't unwind from years of training and combat survival. He became edgy and angry – haunted by memories of the battlefield. His leg slowly healed, but he was burdened with guilt and regret. Going to the grocery store with

145

his wife was a chore he could barely manage without having a panic attack.

His exhausting nightmares threw him back into the exploding ATV beside the severed body of his best friend. Their eyes would meet for an instant of shared terror before, once again, Tom failed to save his dying friend.

The doctor prescribed sedatives and painkillers. And his wife begged him to go to church. He tried, but listening to sermons about doing good acts for others only filled him with guilt. He'd killed three enemy soldiers while on tour. In his dreams, he saw their faces gazing at him innocently – young, alive and full of hope. He couldn't discuss these dreams with anyone because only cowards felt this way.

He'd attended military counseling before returning home. He'd answered the perfunctory questions: no he wasn't planning to kill himself or anyone else. But the therapy process hadn't reached him deep inside where his real wound lived – the endless guilt. By all appearances, he'd behaved bravely. He'd won a medal. He wasn't a coward. But he felt like he shouldn't be alive. Why had he lived? Why not his friend?

"I'm a good person," he would tell himself in the middle of the night, awake from a dream, his heart still pounding. "I went to Iraq for the right reasons. I did as I was trained to do. This is what my father did. Why don't I feel proud? Why can't I stomach the memories? Am I so weak as this?"

He found brief comfort in pain meds prescribed by his doctor. Under the influence of these meds, his memories dimmed. So did all of his feelings: Every emotion became fleeting and painless – including love for his wife and the ambition that once drove him. How long will I feel this way, he asked. No one had an answer. His days only existed on the periphery of his world.

As time went on, his inner pain began to poke through the fog of the pain meds. His leg was healed now. But his inner pain was bursting at the seams of his everyday life. One day it fell apart. He nearly hurt his wife in an argument when his rage got out of hand. He shoved her. She'd become the enemy. She'd threatened him. He exploded. Later, she packed her things and left. "You need help," she said quietly on her way out, looking sad and exhausted.

Months later, in an effort to win his wife back, he attended a veteran support group. Everyone in the room was asked to share a painful memory. One soldier, after telling his story, said: I shouldn't be alive. I don't want to be alive. I'm only causing pain to everyone around me. I've done unspeakable things.

The facilitator began to read something to the group:

Would you consider that you're an old soul or you wouldn't have agreed to participate in war? Only old souls take on the accelerated soul learning that occurs in the heat of battle. When the smoke clears, all that's left for the conscious soldier is to begin again as a wise man, a shaman, a soul healer. He must release the ego - which distorts this world and traps him in indescribable guilt. All that remains from the battlefield is inner wisdom. Logic and purpose have been stripped away. Wisdom is the true essence of the soul. It's born of pain and birthed from pressure like a magnificent diamond forged into existence through torment. This is you now. You must help heal others with your newly birthed wisdom - born from unspeakable pain. Or the lives of others you loved and lost on the field are in vain. You carry their hearts within you.

What are your thoughts on that, asked the facilitator: No one spoke for awhile. Then there was laughter and silliness. "Bunch of shit," said a guy sitting beside Tom. "What's a shaman?" mumbled someone else.

But Tom went home that night pondering those words. Did he feel like he'd grown from the pain of his experiences? Did he feel wiser? Could he look for a different perspective on the suffering he'd endured? Could he help others? How so?

These questions eventually forced him on a journey of exploration outside of his comfort zone. He found books and websites where people exchanged ideas on things he once thought were ridiculous: reincarnation, soul growth, soul agreements. It was all very different from the religious perspective he'd once found so meaningless. He discovered an online forum where ex-military shared their thoughts on soul agreements on the battlefield. He devoured books on psychic phenomenon, remote viewing (once used by the military to spy on other countries) and quantum physics' theory on the nature of energy.

He became obsessed with reading books on everything from the military's use of remote viewing to spy on other countries to the quantum physics' theory that everything is energy. Could he be a soul who came here on purpose? Had he been here before? Did he choose war to evolve his soul? Was his pain on purpose?

After months of study, he shared these books with his wife. He asked her to read some of them. He wanted to talk to her about these new ideas that were changing the way he viewed the world. At first she said no because those ideas were forbidden by her church. But when she realized that he was getting better, she agreed to look at the books that now lined his shelves. They spent many enjoyable evenings having dinner, debating afterlife theories, reincarnation and the value of meditation. They became friends for the first time in a very long while.

Over time, they became better friends than they'd ever been - even though their marriage couldn't be saved. Their journey of exploration led Tom to alternative churches and healing practitioners such as hypnotists and acupuncturists. Eventually with their help, Tom learned to live without pain meds. Years later, he went back to school and become a counselor. He felt ready to help other soldiers heal. The wounded soldier became the healer.

Soul Stories: Maya and Lana

Two children are born into the same circumstances of poverty and abuse. One child, Maya, focuses on the brief and fleeting goodness in an exhausted mother's face, in the smile of a neighbor, the beauty of a butterfly wing.

The other child, Lana, feels only pain, fear, and disappointment. She can't see the brief goodness in a tired mother's smile, or a sudden reflection of light in a neighbor's voice. Yet Lana's life is as filled with angels as Maya's; in the loving visit from a relative who describes a different way of life, and in the soothing conversation with a kind lady working behind a counter.

These are the same angels that Maya sees. But Maya embraces the words of the visiting relative and the lady behind the counter and stashes them in her heart for a future day. She holds onto these words like a beacon in the storm, knowing she'll find her way there someday when the time is right, when the door begins to open. Maya looks for beauty on her walks home. She seeks out the light of a hot summer day, the color of a brief rainbow after a storm. She focuses on these things with her mind, in spite of sadness. She becomes a seeker of beauty in a dark and lonely world.

As Maya's life unfolds, she takes the openings. She embraces the chances that pull her into the light; the conversations with a teacher who believes in her, the kindness of a stranger who gives her a fresh piece of bread everyday. She believes the teacher who says she can do it. She does the work in front of her in spite of the effort it takes to succeed in school when her home is filled with chaos.

Where Maya chooses to hope, Lana chooses not to. When she's told by a supportive teacher to do the work because it will change her life, she doubts it. It's ridiculous to trust, isn't it? She'll stay within the boundaries of what she knows - rather than risk the mistake of reaching for the unknown. Why put out effort for anything when she can sit in the comfort of what she knows. Her fear of change is great.

As Lana grows, her cynicism is affirmed by every sad event that unfolds around her, from abusive boyfriends, to addictions, miserable jobs, illness and poverty. She doesn't understand that even one moment of reaching out for the beauty in a small moment will break her pattern of fear and pull her into the light. The older she gets the harder she has to work to break this cynical pattern, open her heart and trust. Many people will offer opportunities of light and love to help her break this negative cycle. Eventually she'll become one of the awakened ones whether it's late in this lifetime or in another.

Maya, who seeks light and beauty, continues to unfold into her potential. She graduates high school with honors and gets a scholarship to college. She struggles with self-doubt when surrounded by others who've lived such different lives. But her pattern of doing the work and finding the beauty always saves her. She seeks out mentors, supportive teachers and loving adults to guide her. She has learned to trust her inner wisdom - which has always led her away from chaos.

As Maya continues to make choices for light and beauty over darkness, fear and chaos, she moves into a better life. Her new pattern becomes established. And it becomes easier to do the right thing and succeed.

When she briefly struggles with addiction, she fights her way out of it. She does the work. When she finds herself in an abusive relationship, she wakes up one morning and recognizes it. She makes a different choice. Her choices are made from love more often as she aligns with her soul's wisdom. With each lesson, she grows stronger and life gets better.

22

PART TWO HOMEWORK:

How would you view your life from your soul's view?

What moments do you recognize as gifts of opportunity and divine guidance that you did or did not recognize at the time?

Speaking from the soul and not the ego, what would you tell yourself today to inspire yourself to move forward in spite of fear?

Review your past choices from the divine lens perspective and write down the moments when your choices brought you into the light of new and better possibilities and when they didn't.

Look for the pattern in how you make choices and where those choices take you. In the past, when you've chosen from fear, where did those choices get you? When you chose from inspiration and courage, where did those choices get you?

Highlight the moments in your life story when an opening appeared and you took it even though you were afraid, and that choice brought you into a better life.

Practice this technique whenever life feels difficult:

- Take one deep slow breath – follow it in and out.
- Mantra or prayer repetition (Om Namah Shivaya) for several moments.
- Your request: Please help me see my soul's perspective on this challenge.
- I am grateful for…
- I open my heart and send love to…
- This is one positive step I can take today…

A Morning Meditation to Shift into Your Divine Lens:

What is my lesson today divine guides? What is my task? Help me step into the wisdom of my higher self no matter what comes my way.

Show me where the lessons hide today, so that I may acknowledge them, open my heart to them and make choices born of wisdom.

Help me understand what lies beneath my pain. Teach me to hold my truth in awe. Teach me to see the dance of my ego and separate from it.

I'm tired of fighting through painful moments and watching my ego react first. I pray for the instant knowing that comes from my soul's highest truth. I want the divine voice within to be louder than the ego that drives my reactions.

Show me how the ego seeks validation instead of acting in alignment with my soul. Show me the ways I can release this ego, this flawed personality, and stand simply as a naked soul with nothing left to say except "Thank you. I love you."

Give me new vocabulary, paint new memories, release me from my moments of struggle and marinate every piece of me in divine wisdom.

Exercise: Tools to survive the mundane

How can I bring my soul's wisdom, my divine lens, to a day that feels scattered before it even begins? How will I listen to my inner wisdom when I'm stuck in traffic, taking the cat to the vet, going to the dentist or running to a meeting?

Here's how:

Bring your personal "God Guide" with you. This guide will sometimes take the form of Jesus, Buddha, Mother Mary, Laxmi, Nityananda or your departed loved ones. When you remember to do this, you'll feel a powerfully present force of love guiding you with grace.

Consult your personal "God Guide" for what to say when your children challenge you, to calm yourself at the dentist, and for grace when paying bills. Talk out loud to the divine; hold daily conversation with God. Live as if you know that you are divinely guided each step of each day.

Questions to answer:

- Would you feel silly consulting a source of divine guidance throughout your day even while doing errands? Why or why not? Choose one daily task where you will do this such as driving in traffic, grocery shopping, doing laundry or preparing for a meeting.

- Do you feel that your everyday perspective is more in alignment with ego lens or divine lens? Why? What might happen if you shift to divine lens while at work? How might that perspective shift help you?

- Do you feel that your relationships would benefit from the grace of your divine lens perspective? How so? Are you willing to try that?

- Which relationship in particular will you focus on this week and bring your divine perspective to? Make a note in your journal throughout the week about how this relationship is affected or not affected by your shift of perspective.

- What have you learned by shifting lenses in your workplace?

- What have you learned by shifting lenses in your relationships?

Ponder this: Are you a fierce seeker of grace even in the midst of chaos?

Is it possible that within your life today there are moments of love and beauty that you dismiss, although they could change everything? Intend to focus on them.

Do you courageously pursue the wise perspective of your divine lens, which sees light where the ego lens never can? If not, begin today.

Do you courageously pursue the wise perspective of your divine lens even in the midst of chaos, devastating grief or overwhelming fear? If not, ask for divine guidance to begin doing this.

Do you truly understand that just one moment of fierce grace changes everything? Reach for that fierce grace when your heart is heavy, when you feel overwhelmed, when all is lost. Just asking for grace changes everything.

PART THREE:
SWITCHING LENSES: GETTING A NEW
PRESCRIPTION FOR LIFE

23

TOOLS FOR TRANSFORMATION WORKBOOK: YOUR DIVINE LENS WORKBOOK

There are two ways to view our lives...

There are two ways that we mostly view our lives and tell our stories. One is our ego journey, our ego view. I call it the Ego Lens. From this view, life can seem tragic and random and mostly meaningless.

Our other Lens is our Divine Lens. From this view we see the divine order and soul agreements in every event of our lives. From this perspective we remember that we're souls who came here on purpose to evolve and help others evolve. This perspective, although it isn't the popular or most common lens, comes from the soul and is rich with wisdom, forgiveness and healing.

When we lose a loved one, we vacillate between our ego view - which tells us a story of tragic and pointless loss and devastating pain - and our divine view which whispers: All is well. My loved one fulfilled his or her soul mission and made their exit exactly as their soul planned to do.

And when I quiet myself, I can feel and hear and sometimes see them. And when I do this, I know in my heart and soul that they're happy and filled with light and watching over me. I will join them soon enough – as soon as I fulfill my own soul mission here and live like I know they're watching, make them proud of me.

When we wear our Divine Lens, we are ALL capable of connecting to the other side for healing and guidance. When we wear our ego lens we are stuck in the mud here of this heavy energy and lost in our pain.

When we lose a career, we also vacillate between the ego lens which views this loss as a reflection of our unworthiness and of the injustice in the world – and our divine lens which sees this as the opening we've been needing in order to go in a new and more meaningful career direction.

In this moment, I am asking you to trust me and take off your ego lens. Set it down carefully because you will use it again. But for today, I ask you to pick up your divine lens and place it on to see the luminous world that lives all around us and within us.

I will help you adjust your lens and see your soul's story of wisdom and light. And if you'll join me in this perspective, you will experience the healing perspective of your divine lens.

To Determine Which Lens you're wearing today:

Ask yourself:
- How do I feel in my body today?
- Am I feeling love and compassion towards anyone, everyone, myself?
- Do I feel that all is well in the world?
- Am I feeling afraid?
- Do I feel insecure or inadequate in any area of my life?
- Do I feel judged or judgmental?
- Do I feel sad and heavy with grief?
- Do I feel passionate about my work?

All of these questions will let you know which lens you're wearing today.

For example:
- **How do I feel in my body today?**
- Ego Lens answer: heavy, tired, sluggish
- Divine Lens answer: energized, alive, excited

Am I feeling love towards anyone, everyone, myself?
- Ego Lens answer: not really, kinda annoyed at the world and at myself
- Divine Lens answer: feeling compassion towards everyone including myself

Do I feel that all is well in the world?
- Ego Lens answer: No! Things are messed up and people are to blame...
- Divine Lens answer: I see the divine order of everyone's soul journey and realize that we're all awakening to our divinity through pain and love

Sue Frederick's Divine Lens Shifting Workshop

3 Primary Spiritual Principles of Your Divine Lens

1. Practice of meditation to quiet the mind, open the heart, connect to our divinity and hear the voice of our soul.
2. Pain is our fuel: How we shift our perspective to view our greatest pain and use it as our fuel to do our great work and live our best life.
3. Soul agreements and soul missions: We've made soul agreements with all the important players in our life even those who break our hearts. All soul agreements are for our highest good. Learn tools for understanding these agreements as well as for seeing your own great soul potential.

Learn to:

- Quiet the mind to hear your inner wisdom.
- View your life story from the soul's perspective rather than the disempowering ego story.
- Apply that inner wisdom to everyday choices including career.
- Find healing for great losses including the death of a loved one.
- Find purpose in your life and work.
- Use this new perspective to create a plan for moving forward in every area of life.

The Process: 9 Essential Steps To Shift into Your Divine Lens

1. Share Your Ego Story; Explore the difference between Divine Lens and Ego Lens views of your story
2. Explore the Spirituality Question
3. Detox the Poison of Guilt; Explore soul agreements and soul choices made for highest good
4. Feel and Release the Pain: Break Your Heart Wide Open
5. Divine Lens & Reconnection Meditations: Shifting Perspectives
6. Understand Your Soul's Mission & Reinvention Cycles
7. Use Pain as Fuel
8. Share Your Soul Story
9. Shift into Your Divine Lens to Move Forward

Step One: Share Your Ego Story

Write your responses to these questions:
- Tell Me Your Story of Greatest Pain:
- Describe your greatest love & loss, career ups & downs, or childhood abuse:
  - A story of painful loss can't be fully released until it has been fully told.
- Tell or write the story of your loved one's death. Was it sudden? How long was he sick?
- Or tell the story of your greatest career disappointment.
- Or tell the story of your greatest broken heart.

- Or tell the story of your greatest childhood pain.
- Where is the greatest pain in your life right now?
- What would your soul say about why you chose to experience this pain?
- If you're grieving share one of your best memories of your departed loved one or from any moment in your life.
- What would you say to your departed loved one if he were here right now?
- What would he say to you?
- What would your departed loved one want you to do now to fulfill your mission here?
- What soul lesson was your departed loved one teaching you by putting you through this loss?
- What is the purpose of your life – other than financial survival? How can you change your career to more fully align with this more meaningful pursuit?
- Why would your soul (choosing circumstances for your highest good and never out of punishment) have chosen to come here and experience the life you've lived? What were you learning for your highest good?
- What gifts may have been hidden in your moments of greatest pain? These are gifts of awakening that you can only realize now as you review past painful moments:
- What does your greatest self know to be true about using your gifts and talents to make a difference in the world?
- What steps would you take to begin doing that now to make your living?
- What changes would you need to make in your life and in your relationships to move forward?

Step Two: Explore the Spirituality Question

Tell me what you believe in....
- Do you follow a religion or do you have a daily spiritual practice of some kind?
- Share the details of your spiritual journey: How were you raised?
- What do you believe in now?

- Have you explored other religions beyond the one you were raised in?
- Is spirituality a focus of your daily life or not?
- Do you pray or meditate every day? Is so, describe what you do.
- Where do you believe your departed loved ones are now? Where do you believe you'll go when you die?
- Do you believe you're a soul on an intentional journey for your highest good? Why or why not?
- When you're in pain – especially in grief - your most pressing questions are: Why did this loss happen? Where is my loved one now? What is the point of my life now?'

By exploring a broad spiritual (not religious) perspective you may find answers that are truly healing.

This loss is your moment of true spiritual (not religious) awakening. It's calling you to experience first-hand your own divine nature.

Your pain will diminish the instant you have an experience of communicating directly to your departed or to your divine guides and feeling their presence.

You'll have first-hand confirmation that the unseen realms are real.

There's a difference between spirituality and religion. Religion is a set of beliefs and rules governed by a church. If you're already deeply comforted by your church and don't question those beliefs, that's terrific.

If your church's beliefs don't fully resonate with you - are you willing to step out of your comfort zone to explore new ideas & develop your own personal connection to the divine? Write your thoughts:

- To explore this bigger view of spirituality, would you be willing to go on a spiritual journey of exploration?
- Would you consider spending time at a monastery, ashram or spiritual center or taking a meditation class?
- Would you be willing to visit a Hindu and Buddhist Ashram, Unity Church, Science of the Mind Church, Kabala center or read metaphysical books?

This spiritual journey of exploration would help you understand what others believe about the after life and see if those ideas resonate with you.

Write your thoughts on this:

- **Notes on your spiritual journey:**
- What do you believe in spiritually? An afterlife? Heaven?
- What do you believe now?
- How can you bring spirituality more into your day-to-day life?

Suggested books include:

- *Bridges to Heaven: True Stories of Loved Ones on the Other Side* by Sue Frederick;
- *Proof of Heaven* by Eben Alexander, MD;
- *Stroke of Insight* by Jill Bolte Taylor, PhD;
- *The Conscious Universe* by Dean Radin;
- *Science and the Akashic Field* by Laszlo;
- *After We Die, What Then?* by George Meek;
- Movies *What The Bleep Do We Know* & *Something Unknown is Doing We Don't Know What* (award winning documentary).

Step Three: Detox the Poison of Guilt

- If you've lost a career you cared about, what is the guilt story you carry about why this happened?
- If you're grieving a marriage or relationship, what is the guilt story you carry about what you could've done differently?
- If your life hasn't turned out the way you wanted it to, what is the guilt story about why you went off-track?
- **Do you believe our souls choose lessons for our highest good?** Could these losses and disappointments have been perfectly designed to push you to evolve, to live better and love better in the future? What can you do now to become your best self and use this guilt as fuel to move forward?

Grief & Guilt
Whenever someone dies, their loved ones feel guilt. They believe they could have done something more or something different that would have prevented the death.

From a spiritual perspective, death is a soul agreement made before the lifetime begins. There is nothing you or anyone could have done to prevent another soul from departing at their pre-destined time of exit.

Carrying this guilt is like drinking poison everyday and it's not how your loved one wants to see you living. Write your thoughts. Begin by writing your guilt story....

Do you believe our souls choose our lessons?
Carrying guilt is like drinking poison everyday and it's not how your departed loved ones or your divine guides wants to see you living.

From your most spiritual perspective what might have been your soul agreement with your departed? Do you believe our souls choose our exit points from the lifetime? Write your thoughts on this....

Step Four: Feel & Release the Pain

It's necessary to feel your pain in order to release it and heal. This daily meditation is a powerful way to do that. This practice will make you feel better from the first day you try it. I've used it many times in my life and it has helped hundreds of my clients.

The Break Your Heart Wide Open Meditation
1. Start each morning with a ten- to twenty-minute meditation. During this meditation, quiet your mind with mantra or prayer repetition. I repeat the ancient mantra Om Namah Shivaya, a Sanskrit phrase meaning "I bow to the divine self." Or you can repeat the Lord's Prayer.
2. Whenever your thoughts wander into your meditation, gently bring your focus back to the mantra.
3. At the end of the meditation, when your mind has settled down, ask to fully feel and release the pain in your heart.
4. Focus your attention on the heart chakra, take several deep breaths, and allow yourself to deeply experience your

grief. Cry if you need to. To focus the energy, you can place your palm facing upwards in front of your heart.

5. Whenever you feel the pain, picture it leaving your heart chakra and moving out of you, up to the divine source. Give it away to God. See divine beings taking your pain away and transforming it into love. (Picture the pain moving out of your heart as you move your palm away from your heart chakra and up to the divine realms.)

6. Repeat this meditation again at the end of the day before going to sleep. By starting and ending each day with this process, your grief will dissolve and you'll find the energy to move forward with your life.

Step Five: Divine Lens Meditation - Shifting into the Soul's Perspective

Practice this technique whenever life feels difficult:
*   Take one deep slow breath – follow it in and out.
*   Mantra or prayer repetition (Om Namah Shivaya) for several moments.
*   Your request: Please help me see my soul's perspective on this challenge.
*   I am grateful for…
*   I open my heart and send love to…
*   This is one positive step I can take today…

Divine Lens Exercise:

Five steps to shift into your divine lens view:
1. Take a deep slow breath, hold it for five seconds, release the breath slowly through your mouth. Repeat.
2. Send a prayer request for instant wisdom; I pray to be hooked up to the wisdom of my highest self and of the divine realms and the guidance of all the divine beings. I pray to align with this wisdom now and separate from my ego self in order to see this day through my divine lens and choose my words and actions from that perspective.
3. Quiet the mind and open the heart through daily meditation with mantra. Use Om Namah Shivaya. Repeat

this mantra and refocus your mind back to that phrase whenever you notice your thoughts.

4. Learn to see yourself and others as a soul on a shared journey by using tools of compassion such as numerology, astrology, angel cards, and prayer. Say: Help me to see the path my sister/brother walks, understand their pain, and realize how to love them best in their journey – knowing that their limitations and mistakes have nothing to do with me.

5. Ask: What is my next step? How do I move forward through my fear and doubt? Write those questions over and over until you begin to write the answers channeled through from your higher self. You'll know the words are coming from your higher self because you'll be writing quickly without thinking or editing what you write. This is how divine guidance comes to us.

Reconnection: Another Divine Lens Meditation

Over the years I've developed this powerful reconnection technique. It has profoundly helped me — whether I was asking for relief from the pain of grief or needed help in any area of my life. I've seen this technique create incredible healing for my clients & students. I know it will help you too.

When first recovering from grief, practice this at least once a day. If you doubt the connection and don't believe the images and whispers are real, ask your departed for a sign to help you believe. You can ask for flickering lights or a phone call with no one on the other end. Or you can ask to have someone say something to you that day that replicates a phrase you used with your departed.

If you practice this once a day for seven days, it will remove any doubt that your loved one lives on and is still accessible to you. You'll gain a new perspective on your life and see why you're still here. Remember, you have to surrender what you "know" and quiet the logical mind to experience this powerful connection.

- Sit in a quiet space and close your eyes. If it's noisy, use earplugs to create quiet. Take three deep breaths.
- Repeat a high-frequency Sanskrit phrase such as Om Namah Shivaya (I bow to the Divine Self) or repeat the

Lord's Prayer. You can do this quietly in your head. When you notice your thoughts getting in the way, gently bring your focus back to the mantra. I recommend either using this mantra or the Lord's Prayer. You're trying to raise your energy frequency and don't want to attract lost souls. Sanskrit mantras and the Lord's Prayer carry sacred energy and will protect you.

- At the end of fifteen minutes (when you've noticed your mind settling down), stop repeating the mantra and keep your eyes closed. Take a deep breath and open your heart. Send loving energy to your departed. Feel the love and see them feeling it and smiling back at you. Love protects you from anything negative and strengthens your intuition. It opens your connection to the departed.

- Speak directly to your loved one. Repeat their full name three times. Then say, "Hi, are you there?" With your eyes closed, notice the flicker of an image in front of you. Don't fixate on the image or look directly at it. Keep your eyes closed. But be aware that your loved one is taking form for you. Don't be afraid. Concentrate on feeling love in your heart. It enhances your connection and protects you.

- Ask your most pressing questions. Examples: Will I find love? Will I find work? Should I sell the house? Can you help me feel stronger? Why am I still here? Why did you have to go? What should I do now? Can you help ease my pain?

- Then be quiet and listen. They're speaking to you. You may doubt it because it will feel as if you're imagining the conversation. You're not. This is how they communicate. If you're feeling cynical, tell yourself, "Okay this is a fun game of imagination..." But stick with it. Take note of everything they say, the ideas that pop into your head, and the images you get. This is all guidance for you.

- Send them gratitude! Say, "Thank you for your help! I feel your presence and I appreciate it!"

- Write down any ideas, phrases, images, or feelings you received or that come to you now upon reflection.

- Get up and go about your day. Later take time to reflect on what you experienced. Contemplate how the guidance applies to your life. Write about your experience with this technique:

Protection Technique:

Love is the most powerful positive force of all and it always trumps darkness. When you're afraid, send love to what you fear. It's like turning on a light in a dark room. Open your heart and pump the love. Darkness will disappear.

When you're afraid, this will help you: Sit in meditation until you can feel love for just one person in your life. See that person wrapped in your powerful love. Pump the love to this person until you see them smiling and laughing.

Now extend that love energy out to the entire space around you filling it with golden light. Now pump your love out to the entire world. See our planet wrapped in golden love and light, and all of its people looking peaceful and happy. Spend time with that image. When you open your eyes, the room you're sitting in will shimmer with love and light. Your fear will be gone.

Remembering Your Intuition

Describe moments in your life when you've felt intuitive or had intuitive experiences and dreams:

Did you trust the information you received? Why or why not? What did you learn from these intuitive experiences?

As a child, were your intuitive experiences encouraged or dismissed by your family of origin?

When does your intuition show up most powerfully?

When your loved one died did you feel him/her communicating with you?

Have you felt his presence in your life since he died? How so?

Describe any dreams you've had that may have been a message from your departed:

Ask Yourself…

Does your current circle of friends and partners embrace or dismiss intuition?

If you have not felt your departed's presence could it be because your grief and pain has been so intense that it blocked the communication?

Are you willing to do the Break Your Heart Wide Open Meditation to release your pain and then try connecting to your departed?

Are you willing to do the Reconnection Meditation to experience first-hand the presence of your departed loved one?

Write your thoughts on this:

Intuitive Living Meditation:

Practice your intuition every day. Before heading home from work ask: "Should I take this route or the other route?" Now close your eyes and see yourself on one of the possible routes home and note how your body feels. Do you get a good or bad feeling in response to seeing that particular drive? If it's good, take that route home.

Afterwards, reflect on how the commute went for you. Was it easier than usual? Was there less traffic?

Plan an intuitively guided vacation. Visit a new city and plan your activities each morning based on your gut feelings. Keep a journal of how this works for you.

As you learn to trust your intuition for these little everyday choices, you'll be better able to trust your intuition for the big life choices. And the more confident you'll become about communicating with the departed.

Step Six: Understanding Your Soul's Mission & Reinvention Cycles

Once you find your path, you understand your soul's mission and what you came to do. It reveals your Great Work for this lifetime.

Your path illuminates your reason for being here in the physical world even though your loved one has moved on and/or even though you may have lost many things you care about.

By embracing the soul's mission, you rise to the challenge of your lifetime and fulfill your purpose. Only then are you able to join your loved one in the highest realms.

You have to know who you are and why you're still here; this empowers you to focus on the future, move through pain and fulfill your mission (which is the reason you're here).

Your Birth Path
Understanding your soul journey through the numbers in your date of birth:

Take the numbers of your day, month and year of birth and add them together to arrive at a single digit. For example:

Sept = 9
15 = 6
1951 = 16 = 7

9 + 6 + 7 = 22 = 4

Another Example of Birth Path Calculation
Birth Date: October 16, 1980
Month = October equals 10, equals 1 (1+0=1)
Date = 16 equals 7 (1 + 6 = 7)
Year = 1980 equals 9
9 = (1 + 9 + 8 + 0 = 18) (1 + 8 = 9)
Total of month (1) plus date (7) plus year (9) equals 17, - which equals 8 (8 = 1 + 7)
Birth Path = 8 (1+7+9=17=8)

The Master Soul Numbers
The master numbers of 11, 22, and 33 represent sacred birth paths that we can choose when we're ready to take on the task of helping humanity evolve. Those numbers are not reduced to a single digit in the final birth path calculations. (But they are reduced to single digits when calculating your final sum. For example, the month of November digits down to a 2 to determine your birth path number.)

Example of a Master Soul Birth Path Calculation
Birth Date: September 15, 1951
Month = September equals 9
Date = 15 equals 6 (1+5 = 6)
Year = 1951 equals 7
7 = (1 + 9 + 5 + 1 = 16), (1+6)
Total of month (9) plus date (6) plus year (7) equals 22
Total = 22 master path soul (9 + 6 + 7 = 22)

This is also referred to as a 22/4 path since the 22 is always connected to the 4 path. Similarly, the 11 path is referred to as 11/2 path, and the 33 path is referred to as a 33/6 path.

3 Ways of Adding Birthdates

It's important to add each birth date three different ways to check your addition and to look for hidden master path numbers.

This is especially important if you've arrived at a 2, 4, or 6 birth path calculation. These birth paths often contain a hidden 11, 22, or 33 path if added two other ways. If the master soul number is "hidden" in this way, it means this person will choose when they're ready to step up to their great work – usually later in life.

Example:

Birth Date: May 1, 1960

These are the three ways you would add this birth date to discover that two out of three ways reveal a 22/4 path while the third way reveals a 13/4.

Traditional Method #1

May = 5 = 5
1 = 1 = 1
1960= 7 = +7
         13 = 4

Second Method

5
1
+1960
1966=22/4 (1 + 9 + 6 + 6 = 22)

Third Method

5 + 1 + 1 + 9 + 6 + 0 = 22/4

170

Another Example:
Birth Date: Sept 15, 1951
Traditional Method #1
Birth date: Sept 15, 1951
September = 9
15 = 6
1951 = 7
Total = 22 (9 + 6 + 7 = 22)

Second Method
Birth date: Sept 15, 1951
1951
     15
    +9
1975 = 22 (1 + 9 + 7 + 5 = 22)

Third Method
Birth date: Sept 15, 1951
9 + 1 + 5 + 1 + 9 + 5 + 1 = 31 = 4 (3 + 1 = 4)

Calculate your birth path from your date of birth using all three of the methods displayed above:
First method result:

Second method result:

Third method result:

All three methods should arrive at the same final number--even if you discover you're on a master soul path of 11, 22, or 33. Those master soul path calculations result in the consistent final combinations of 11/2, 22/4, or 33/6 --at least one of the ways you add the birth date. The other two ways may result in various other two-digit numbers that when added together total 2, 4 or 6. (Examples are 20/2, 13/4 or 15/6).

Your birth month:

Your birth date:

Your birth year:

Total:

Reduced to a single digit:

Your birth path number:

Note: Zero is more than a placeholder in numerology. It's called a potentiator--meaning the zero makes the number in front of it (or behind it) stronger. If your birth-path calculation arrives at the number 2020, each zero strengthens the two in front of it–making this number digit down to a 22/4 master path. The same is true for 1010 or 3030, which become 11/2 and 33/6.

Now read the brief descriptions below to begin to understand the lessons and challenges you selected for this lifetime and the soul mission you intended to fulfill:

If your single digit final number from your date of birth is:

1. You came here to learn to believe in your uniqueness, to follow your inner voice and authentic vision no matter what anyone thinks of you or expects of you. You'll have events and relationships that cause you to doubt yourself. But your life mission is to use that self-doubt as your fuel to become a great leader and visionary capable of changing the world. This will unfold once you trust your inner wisdom, slip on your divine lens and do work that helps others find their uniqueness and overcome their self-doubt.

2. You have a gift for connecting to others with empathy and intuitive awareness. You're an healer as long as you don't let your sensitivity wound you. When you're focused on organizing the details of life you're hiding from your true self, running from your powerful inner wisdom, and not stepping up to your great work. (If the addition of your birth date numbers ended in 11/2 – even just one of the three ways you can add it – this means you're on the 11 master soul path. Please read about this further on.)

3. You have a brilliant, creative mind and are a gifted communicator through written and spoken words, movement, and other forms of creative expression. You're a rule breaker, on purpose. Meant to be an entrepreneur, you must launch that business, write that book, open your movement or healing studio, and make your living from your self-expressive path. Your challenge is to quiet the mind and open your heart - which is difficult because you've learned to trust your ideas and not your gut. To fulfill your mission, you'll need to

change that pattern and learn to carry the heart of healing within you.

4. You're strong, responsible, and determined. Your inner strength and your physical strength will save your life and guide you in the right direction. Use your hard work to create new systems and foundations for the world's problems. Your passion for truth must be the guiding force for the work you do. Think bigger than just the task in front of you and nothing will stop your success. (If the addition of your birth date numbers ended in 22/4 – even just one of the three ways you can add it – this means you're on the 22 master soul path. Please read about this further on.)

5. You came into this lifetime to fearlessly embrace the physical world and fully experience the joys, challenges and lessons of living in a body. Your body will be the vehicle for most of your lessons and your gifts here. You're charismatic and will attract everything you want; the lesson is learning to pick from higher self, from divine lens and not ego lens. Courage is your guide in every challenge and it's what you came to learn. Step away from conventional careers, fear-based religions, and empty relationships to find your authentic self. Center yourself and overcome addictions with disciplined spiritual practice. Much of your lifetime does not require effort. But your spiritual work is necessary. Putting effort into meditation and spiritual studies will allow you to accomplish what you came here to do.

6. You carry the heart of the compassionate healer and you care greatly for those around you, family, community, and the world at large. You sense what others needs and always want to help them. But losing yourself in the needs of others will poison your heart and pull you away from your own divinity. Your unique path to the divine must come first. Channel in your artistic gifts, your intuitive knowingness, and use your brilliance to align with sacred self rather than your lower self. Then you can save the world as you intended to do. (If the addition of your birth date numbers ended in 33/6 – even just one of the three ways you can add it – this means you're on the 33 master soul path. Please read about this further on.)

7. You're deeply sensitive and intuitive and yet you also have an amazing analytical mind. When you use your brilliant mind to pursue spiritual knowledge (not religion) you'll find your truth. Then you can teach the world a better way to live. You can use science, nature or the arts as your path to wisdom. But all paths must lead to spiritual solutions or your cynicism will destroy your life.

8. You came to learn the lesson of power: how to own it fully in every area of your life – spiritual, physical, emotional, and financial. You intended to use that power to do good work in the world. Once you embrace this challenge and stop hiding from it, you'll find your way and become more successful and wealthy than most. But your wealth and power must eventually be used to empower others. It's what you came here to do and the lesson you came to learn.

9. You're a wise old soul who chose this path to tie up the loose ends of your spiritual evolution. You agreed to face many losses and disappointments in this lifetime because your soul is ready to pass the test; to step into wisdom, compassion and forgiveness no matter what pain you feel. If you're avoiding your mission, you'll use your charismatic personality and many accomplished skills to manipulate and diminish others. This will leave you empty, alone and broken. When you embrace the path of wisdom, you'll become the spiritual bridge between this world and the next.

11/2 – You carry extraordinary sensitivity and beauty within, and you have a direct, wide-open channel to the divine. You're meant to use that as your gift – to see the pain of others (not just yourself) and use your intuition to heal and inspire the world. If you let your sensitivity wound you, you can be paranoid and rage-full – which is not who you came here to be. But the moment you quiet your mind, open your heart, and deepen your spiritual pursuits, your life unfolds beautifully.

22/4 – You agreed to get it done in the way it needs to get done in order to shift consciousness here on earth. Your mission requires hard work; studying, writing, teaching, creating media and living boldly in the world. You're perfectly designed for this task and you brought with you all the strength and courage you need to get it done. When you step up to the challenge, your work will make a great difference in the world - helping consciousness evolve.

33/6 – You're a pure, high vibrational channel to the divine. You can open your heart and understand the essence of humanity and its struggles. Your intention is to use this wide-open channel to bring in your gifts of wisdom, beauty, inspiration and spiritual awareness to help the world. You walk the path of the compassionate intuitive healer, yet if you don't embrace your inner wisdom, your sensitivities can lead to addictions and mental illness. Choosing your divine lens will save your life and allow you to then save the world.

Based on this Birth Path information that helps you understand the life plan you created for yourself before this lifetime began, what steps would you take moving forward to align your life and career with your soul mission:

How would you view the challenges you face today through the wisdom of what you came to learn on your Birth Path:

Personal Year Cycles
All of your life you've experienced repeated nine-year cycles of reinvention. By understanding where you are now in your reinvention cycles, you can more gracefully heal your life, embrace your true work and see life from your soul's perspective – through your Divine Lens.

Every year of your life you've been under the influence of a particular number – 1 through 9, 11, 22 or 33. You're working with a different type of energy each year within a repeating nine-year cycle. These nine-year cycles are designed to move you through cycles of necessary reinvention and loss; helping you master the challenges you signed up for and accomplish the work you came here to do.

You began this lifetime under the influence of the birth-path number you chose. If that number is 3, then the first year of your life was a 3 personal year. The second year of your life was a 4 personal year, and so on.

Your current personal year is determined by the single-digit numbers of your birth month and birth date added to the current calendar year and reduced to a single digit or master number.

Example:

Birthdate: Sept 15, 1951

Month: Sept = 9

Date: 15 = 6

Current Year: 2012 = 5

9 + 6 + 5 = 20 = 2

Personal year: 2

Calculate your Personal Year:

Your Birth Month:

Your Birth date:

Current year:

Total:

Reduced to a single digit:

This is your Personal Year:

Meaning of the Personal Years

Personal Year 1

It's a year to focus on YOU. It's time to launch your business, get a new job or title, start a graduate program, or move to a new location. Everything you do this year will influence the events of your life for the next nine years. If you don't plant seeds for a better future now, nothing will come to bloom as this cycle unfolds. Tap into all the new energy that will help you release the past and reinvent. There's never been a better time for taking steps toward your ultimate dream. Everything revolves around you and is dependent upon you. Believe in your vision, make important decisions alone, and move forward bravely--like a pioneer.

Personal Year 2

This is your year for connecting deeply with others. Your career won't be all on your shoulders anymore as new partners step forward to offer support for the project you started last year. It's a slower, sweeter year, one in which you nurture what you've already started rather than pushing hard to launch new things. Success hinges on opening your heart, trusting your heightened intuition, and saying yes to collaboration. It's important to be receptive. Soften the forceful energy you thrived on last year. You might feel highly sensitive now, but don't let this get in the way of love. Your solution is to become the source of love for others-- even when you're feeling wounded.

Personal Year 11

This is a highly charged year of personal illumination and intellectual achievement. You'll be inspired to heal the relationships in your life and accomplish your most inspired work. Your intuition, inspiration, and artistic creativity are magnified and so is your sensitivity. Daily meditation or prayer will enhance all of your gifts and reinforce your connection to the divine. That spiritual connection is more powerful than ever this year. Use it as your source for actions. Spend time with highly evolved, conscious people who inspire you to create. Small talk and meaningless social engagements will drain you because of your heightened sensitivity. This is your best year for developing spiritual, intuitive, and artistic gifts as well as learning to love in a profoundly new way.

Personal Year 3

This is the fun, sexy, playful year to create projects for your new work. Express yourself, get into the center of things, join social groups, and entertain. Forget long-term planning and just enjoy life; don't make important decisions about your future. Develop your skills with words--written and spoken. Life is your stage-- enjoy it! Whatever you started in your 1 year through hard work and diligence is now reaping enjoyment for you. It's a year to blossom.

Personal Year 4

It's time to focus on your great work. Just get it done. Focus on being responsible to your career and tapping into core strengths whenever challenged. It's a serious year to fulfill obligations, get practical and organized, and build the foundation for future growth. Create your budget and do the physical work. Get your home in order--whether that means moving, remodeling, or cleaning. Get in shape physically and cultivate strength in all areas of life. Dependability, honesty, and responsibility are required in relationship and career.

Personal Year 22

This is your best year for manifesting inspired work in the world. Anything is possible! Ignoring your work will leave you feeling off-balance, unfocused, and useless. Use inspiration as your fuel to get it all done. Don't waste a moment going on long vacations (you won't be able to relax). Focus on your great work and trust that love and relaxation will come later. This is a year for putting personal concerns aside and doing your best for the world at large. Make big plans and introduce changes. You'll have the opportunity to ascend to your greatest career achievements and acquire abundant financial rewards. You'll also feel the sting of criticism that greatness attracts. Focus on your work and keep moving forward.

Personal Year 5

This year, your charisma is amped up and your magnetism is attracting everyone--from potential partners to new business opportunities. Hold steady to your true self or you'll get pulled off path. Be open, fearless, passionate, and free. You'll have opportunities for expansion, adventure, and the unexpected in this turning-point year. Everything is vibrant and changing around you. Take trips (it's time for that long vacation), investigate career opportunities, and get rid of anything or anyone that holds you back. Make room for the new. Focus on freedom and adapting to change. Enjoy this sensual year with good food, relationships, and trips to exotic places. You'll be super-charged, attractive, and sexual. You can revive tedious relationships or work circumstances with your new energy and charisma.

Personal Year 6

This year is time of deep love and nurturing. Focus on commitment, family, and responsibility. Your heart opens wide to embrace others. Rather than focus on yourself, adjust to the needs of others. Shift away from the passionate excesses of the 5 personal year. Relationships will blossom as you nurture them with your new open-hearted energy. Reach out to understand the people in your life. Let go of superficiality and take responsibility for others. Yet don't take on more than you can carry, or you'll fall into depression and be overwhelmed. This is one year, though, when general harmony is more important than your own needs.

Personal Year 33

You'll be drawn to mystical knowledge, intuition, and spiritual guidance this year. But if you're not grounded, you could become disconnected to everyday reality. Stay away from alcohol and drugs, and meditate every day. If you embrace your higher self, it will be your most inspired year artistically. You'll channel in genius--whether you're an actor, musician, or artist. Your pipeline to the divine is opened up and flowing freely with spiritual and creative inspiration. Take a meditation retreat and create, create, create! Your finished product and enlightened ideas will change the world.

Personal Year 7

This is a time for deep reflection, intuitive development, and spiritual growth. Sign up for a meditation and yoga retreat together. Take meditation classes and spend a weekend in prayer and silence. Strength will only come from your connection to the divine. You may feel a bit lonely or isolated, whether you're in a relationship or not. Use your alone time to write a book, research higher consciousness, or take a psychology class. Focus on finding your true purpose. Withdraw from the center of things; superficial social events won't feel good. Your sensitivity and intuition is elevated, and you'll pick up other people's feelings everywhere you go. Refine what you started in this nine-year cycle by analyzing and perfecting projects and relationships. Your intuition will be at its most powerful--rely on it for all decisions. Pursue nothing--you'll naturally attract what is meant to be in your life.

Personal Year 8

Money and career will be the topic of nearly every conversation. You'll have many opportunities to make money and advance your career and that should be your focus. It's a year to go to the bank--not the bar. Even when you go out partying, your mind will be home crunching numbers to see how you can improve your business or pay off your debts. It's time to own your power both financially and physically. Get back into shape--financially and physically. If you wrote a book last year, this is the year to promote and sell it. If you researched and developed your new business last year, now is the time to get it funded. Physical accomplishment and material success are your focus, as you reap the seeds of success that you planted early in this nine-year cycle. During this powerful year, take command to get results. Think big, manage and direct others, move forward. Beware of abusing your power in relationships. Be patient and generous to others-- even if that feels tedious.

Personal Year 9

It's time to clean house, to surrender what you no longer need and what holds you back. Friends and lovers from the past will resurface to be examined, then kept or discarded for the next cycle. Your career will conclude the focus that it has had for the past nine years, even though you won't see the new cycle just yet. Open your hands and let go, with faith that something new and better will arrive in your 1 year. You may even be fired or laid off. Relationships will fall away or be transformed, and you'll grieve for your losses over the past nine years. Peace comes from higher wisdom and a greater connection to spirituality. Your insights and wisdom will be heightened. Use this awareness to benefit the people around you. Focus on artistic and spiritual disciplines, and wait for the new inspiration that begins soon in your approaching 1 year.

Map Your Own Reinvention Cycles

One of the most helpful steps of understanding your Soul Story is looking through all of your previous nine-year cycles and discussing what was going on during each cycle. Starting with your birth year, write each year of your life to the left of the personal year number you were experiencing. Also include your age.

Make notes by the years when important events occurred-- especially note when relationships and careers began or ended, and when you experienced grief and loss.

Note any changes that took place when one nine-year cycle ended and a new one began. Note what you learned about yourself during the Saturn Return.

By examining your past reinvention cycles what insights do you have about your current challenge and moving through it? What insights have you gained from reviewing your cycles?

Ask Yourself...
- How did each 9 year cycle begin and end?
- What was my intention at beginning of each cycle?
- What did I let go of at end of each cycle?
- When did I fall in or out of love? When did I start and end careers?
- When did I have children or long to have children?
- When did my loved one die?
- What did I learn?
- What did I learn about myself during the Saturn Return?
- When I look at my Saturn Returns what can I learn about the purpose of my pain and how it fuels my life and great work?

Saturn Returns
At the ages of 28 and 29, you go through your First Saturn Return. This is a major transition point of the lifetime--your first true wake up moment of recognizing your journey for this lifetime and what it's really about. You'll see that your life is going to turn out differently from how you thought it would be. And you'll understand that you're not here to meet the expectations of family and friends. This is your moment of seeing who you really are. You may lose a career or lose someone you love at this transition point - whether it's a parent, friend or spouse. Or you may lose a career or reinvent your career at this point. All loss is meant to fuel your reinvention.

At the ages of 58 and 59, you go through your Second Saturn Return. This is the second major transition point of your lifetime--where you're stripped naked until you finally become your true self in the world. You're no longer allowed to hide behind limiting job titles or relationships. It's time to be the authentic self you came here to be--doing your great work in the world. This is also a time when you may lose someone you love or lose a career or a relationship and use pain to fuel your reinvention.

Step Seven: Use Pain as Fuel

Consider the possibility that all of your pain--every wound you've ever experienced, from loss to illness to disappointment--was exactly what you needed and chose in order to arrive at this point in your life, which is exactly where you're supposed to be.

Imagine that your soul chose to experience loss to open your heart and strengthen your connection to the divine--to push you onto your true path and inspire you to accomplish your soul's greatest mission.

Your greatest work offers to the world what you wish had been offered to you in your moment of greatest pain.

Consider this....

Grief fuels your greatest spiritual & emotional reinvention; it breaks your heart wide open & sends you searching for the truth of where your loved one went and/or why you're still here.

Grief brings a clarity and focus to your life's purpose that gives you a powerful advantage in everything you do.

Grief will drive you to see beyond the surface and embrace a truly spiritual perspective in every area of your life.

Our losses heal us by giving us a chance to refocus on what's important, truly love the people still in our lives & find the great work that fulfills our mission & answers the question 'why am I still here?'

Write your thoughts on this & how it might apply to your life:

Tell or write the story of your loved one's death or your career or relationship loss. In the story answer these questions:
- What soul lesson was your departed loved one teaching you by putting you through this loss?
- What would your departed want you to do with your life now?
- If you knew your departed was here beside you, what would you say to him? What would he say to you?
- From your most spiritual perspective, what has been the gift of this experience?

- If you've lost a career, what gifts could be hidden in this change of direction?
- If you've lost a relationship what positive attributes about yourself have you discovered?
- What three steps are you willing to take to bring a more powerfully spiritual perspective into your daily life and work?
- What steps are you willing to take to use your pain as fuel to accomplish your soul's greatest mission?

Step Eight: Share Your Soul Story

How would you view your life from your soul's view?

What moments do you recognize as gifts of opportunity and divine guidance that you did or did not recognize at the time?

Speaking from the soul and not the ego, what would you tell yourself today to inspire yourself to move forward in spite of fear?

Review your past choices from the divine lens perspective and write down the moments when your choices brought you into the light of new and better possibilities and when they didn't.

Look for the pattern in how you make choices and where those choices take you. In the past, when you've chosen from fear, where did those choices get you? When you chose from inspiration and courage, where did those choices get you?

Highlight the moments in your life story when an opening appeared and you took it even though you were afraid, and that choice brought you into a better life.

At each lesson or painful moment in your life, ask yourself why your soul chose that lesson and what you were trying to learn to further your soul's evolution.

Five baby steps to practice daily:
1. Meditation
2. Deep breathing in a moment of fear or anger
3. The Divine Lens Meditation: Shifting into the Soul's Perspective
4. Stepping back from crisis for 5 seconds to listen to inner wisdom
5. Leaning into the pain to see the lesson of it

Take out a notebook and pen and get seated comfortably. Spend a few minutes quieting your mind through meditation.

Take a deep breath and ask for divine guidance.

Say: Please help me see my journey as I intended to fulfill it here – living with wisdom, love and light.

Now begin writing your story in third person as if you're telling a story about someone other than yourself. Begin with childhood and observe the main painful and happy lessons of that time in your life and how you rose above them with grace and forgiveness. Move to the launching of career and show how you used your pain and gifts to create work that inspired the world or could have done so.

Explain how you helped others and fulfilled your soul's mission or could have done so. Write about the relationships you attracted both painful and wonderful and ultimately the love you embraced or did not embrace. Write about the graceful exit of your death as your soul has planned it for you. Write quickly so that it pours through from your right brain, your intuition, your soul.

Now take another breath and ask for more wisdom. Read through your story keeping in the painful challenges that you've faced but filling in your steps after those challenges with even more love and wisdom at every turn until you tell the story of your richest most fulfilled potential lifetime. When it feels right to you, keep it. **This is now your story. The only one you'll ever tell again.**

Step Nine: Divine Lens Shifters

Focus on one thing in your life you can feel grateful for right now. Keep focusing on it as if you are wearing binoculars and exploring it up close. See each detail of what you're grateful for. Now open your heart and send that one object or person you're grateful for a big burst of love. Wrap them in compassion. You've now shifted into your divine lens. Focus your divine lens on the challenge you're currently facing, and send compassion to the people who are troubling you.

Take a deep breath with a long inhale and long exhale. Say: Please divine guides show me the lesson of this moment and reveal the divine lens view of this story I'm telling myself today.

Pull me out of the ego view and show me the wisdom of this lesson. Write your thoughts on this:

When I look back at this difficult moment in my life how will I think of it? How will I wish I had handled this challenge from my most enlightened compassionate perspective? Looking back at this moment in your life, describe your soul story of how you gracefully overcame this challenge by choosing love over fear:

Use these Energy Shifters daily to shift into Your Divine Lens
- Open Your Heart: Love Recklessly
- Refocus Your Thoughts
- Tell A New Story
- Shift from Superficial to Super-Spiritual
- Laugh Like There's No Tomorrow
- Forgive With Abandon
- Get Wildly Grateful
- Sweeten Up
- Move Your Chi
- Feed Your Chi
- See Your Best Future

Share one thing that you're grateful to have in your life now:
Just focusing on that one thing will help you shift your energy to a higher frequency and allow healing to happen.

Share one thing that you're grateful for about this painful loss:

Start each day by saying out loud something you're grateful for, and then repeat it again before bedtime. Gratitude is a potent energy shifter that will make you feel better instantly.

By using these energy shifters every day you regain control of your life and regain your happiness.

Give examples of how you might bring these energy shifters into your life more often:

5 steps in 3 months:
List 5 steps you'll take in the next 3 months to shift into your Divine Lens, fulfill your soul's mission, use your pain as fuel, & live as if you know your departed loved one is watching you & that all relationships even the ones that hurt you are soul agreements for your highest good:

After taking all of these Nine Steps to Shift into your Divine Lens what have you learned about your most prevalent view of your life? Do you most often use the Ego Lens view? Do you feel comfortable shifting into your Divine Lens more often?

Just taking a few of these baby steps can make a major shift for the better. Are you willing? Let's do this....

About the Author

Sue Frederick is the author of *Bridges to Heaven: True Stories of Loved Ones on the Other Side; I See Your Soul Mate & I See Your Dream Job (St. Martin's Press)*. An intuitive since childhood, Sue draws upon decades of spiritual study and practice, and powerful inner wisdom to help her clients and students fulfill their soul's mission, access their divine lens and use their pain as fuel for a meaningful life. Sue has trained more than 500 intuitive coaches around the world. Her work has been featured in the New York Times, CNN.com, Real Simple, Yoga Journal, Natural Health and Complete Woman Magazines. She's been a guest on more than 200 radio shows and numerous TV shows including Bridging Heaven & Earth.

For more information visit www.SueFrederick.com or
www.YourDivineLens.com
Email: Sue@Brilliantwork.com
303-939-8574

60906896R00120

Made in the USA
Charleston, SC
08 September 2016